ACCLAIM FOR
UNSHAKABLE INNER PEACE

This is a ground-breaking book on how spiritual development works. Follow Rachael Jayne's real-time journey from struggles with fear and rejection to awakening. Her quest for inner peace will guide you through the steps to embody a steadfast feeling of safety and trust in life.

– SARA YAGOUB BROWN, HOST OF
RENEGADE REVOLUTION RADIO.

Rachael Jayne has triumphed again with *Unshakable Inner Peace*. It's not easy to be vulnerable and brutally honest towards ourselves and reveal our deepest secrets for the world to see, but Rachael Jayne manages to do both. This book is a fantastic template for self-inquiry, transformation, and enlightenment. I found myself using the practices and experiences as I read her book, and I am walking away with new tools to help me observe and shift what I thought was my indomitable ego self. I highly recommend this for anyone on a spiritual journey.

– JAMES KAWAINUI, NATIVE HAWAIIAN HEALER,
BEST-SELLING AUTHOR AND SPIRITUAL STRATEGIST.

I was so moved. This was not like reading a book, this was like I was in a spiritual experience myself, expanding and letting go with every word on the page. Rachael Jayne has a gift for simplifying the complexities of spirituality into a practical way of embracing life.

– Denise Bonanni,
Master Teacher of Art of Feminine Presence®.

I get it now! This book clarified spiritual concepts I have heard for years but could only partially understand. I'm inspired and forever changed by reading this book. My mind is less worried and more joyful. This book will remain by my side. Thank you, Rachael Jayne!

– Amy Kennedy, Artist, Creator of the EVOLVE Mentoring Program For Visual Artists.

With exquisite presence and raw authenticity, Rachael Jayne shares with us a pristine roadmap to finding and sustaining inner peace. She walks us through the minefields of spiritual bypass, denial, and resistance, leading us gently and assuredly along a simple and elegant path to profound self-awareness, acceptance, and love. Highly recommended, this is a must-read for every person on a spiritual journey of awakening.

– Ashana, Crystal Bowl Artist, Musician,
and Best-Selling Author.

UNSHAKABLE INNER PEACE

Get off the Mental and Emotional Rollercoaster for Good

Book One of the Unshakable Series

RACHAEL JAYNE GROOVER

Deep
Pacific
Press

Published by Deep Pacific Press
117 E 37th St. #580, Loveland, Colorado 80538
(970) 377 - 2562

Deep
Pacific
Press

Unshakable Inner Peace / Rachael Jayne Groover – 1st ed.
ISBN: 978-1-956108-22-4 (paperback)
ISBN: 978-1-956108-23-1 (ebook)
Library of Congress Control Number: 2023947729

Cover design: Patrick Knowles
Interior design & formatting: Mark Thomas / Coverness.com

PROGRAMS & RETREATS
BY RACHAEL JAYNE GROOVER

Art of Feminine Presence®

Art of Masculine Presence®

Spiritual & Successful®

Awaken Your Impact®

Unshakable Certainty

Unshakable Transformation

The Awakened Business School®

The Inspired Writer®

DEDICATED

*To all in The Awakened School® community
who've embraced sitting in the fire with me,
choosing courage over comfort.
You inspire my growth and service.*

Contents

INNER PEACE

I walked on stage when it was my turn. The leader of the speaker training sat in front, ready to evaluate my performance, looking just like a judge from America's Got Talent. I had already spoken in front of tens of thousands of people and led dozens of seminars in massive ballrooms. I felt solid in my ability to speak in public, and I was there to get better.

I spent hours preparing for this three-minute time on stage and looked forward to trying out some new material. The audience gave me solid eye contact. They were attentive and laughed when I wanted them to. When the timer sounded, I felt confident while awaiting my feedback.

"Never do that again," the speaker trainer growled. "You should *never* make fun of anyone in your speech. It's rude and unprofessional."

Confused, I replied, "I didn't intentionally make fun of anyone. I meant it as light-hearted humor."

"Well, don't ever do it again on my stage," she said, as if I were a five-year-old.

I stared at her with a shocked expression.

"You should know better, Rachael Jayne. I'm surprised you failed to hit the mark on this one, given your experience as a speaker." I felt like a spanked five-year-old.

My face hot, I walked back to my seat, my mind foggy. My body flipped between anger, sadness, and humiliation. The next speaker received similar treatment. No encouraging words. No, "You did such and such well." No inspiring narrative to help someone improve. She made Simon Cowell look like a teddy bear. I watched four more people get torn down. It made me sick, and I left.

I was furious by the time I got back to my hotel room. I looked at myself in the bathroom mirror and wound myself into the ugliest cry imaginable. Everything I had been teaching about staying peaceful and present for fifteen years sailed down the toilet. No amount of breathing into my core could help me regain my center.

I knew I wanted unshakable inner peace and had occasionally experienced it as a side effect of two decades of inner work and meditation. However, my critical, seeking, and comparing mind was active most of the time and would shove me out of that experience.

What shoves you off *your* peaceful path? What does it take for you to get triggered by someone? Do you recognize any of these states of mind?

- ► A mind that judges yourself and others.
- ► A doubting mind that stops you from doing what your heart calls you to do.
- ► A mind that says you're never good enough when comparing yourself to others.
- ► A mind that's never satisfied and quickly disappointed.
- ► A mind that holds on too tight—so much so that it pushes people away.
- ► A catastrophic mind that focuses on the worst-case scenario and is afraid of change.

Are any of these states of mind playing their tunes in your head— even though you've already worked on yourself? If so, *Unshakable*

Inner Peace is for you. This book is about escaping the cycle of mental and emotional suffering into an unwavering place of strength and peace. The official psycho-spiritual term for this is, getting off the "Oh sh*t! rollercoaster." On this ride called life, some days we're screaming, "I'm not up for this!" On other days it's, "Is it safe to be this happy?" Fear of the unknown, fear of judgment, fear that nothing will change—it's all part of the human experience, but it's the spiritual experience that brings the lasting relief we all seek.

Unshakable Inner Peace is a book for those committed to their personal and spiritual development who want to be a beacon of light for others. It's for those who want to significantly reduce anxiety and fearful thought patterns and receive clear, intuitive guidance on their next direction. It's for those who want to stay tuned to infinite possibilities during uncertain times—which lately seem more intensely uncertain than ever.

Your spiritual path, religion, and belief systems are not important to me on our journey together. I welcome all traditions. This conversation is not about a particular spiritual ideology, but how to unwind the contracted mind, heart, body, and energy field to experience unshakable peace, love, power, and knowing.

With *Unshakable Inner Peace* you're about to read what unfolded within me in real time. Somehow or other, I found space to write 12,000 words daily for four days straight, while the most incredible transformation had its way with me. It was as if time slowed for me to capture in words the micro-movements of that awakening. A voice with precision, compassion, and humor arrived as a mentor, with intelligence far beyond my own, to coach me through my false assumptions and tightly held ego. We had a meaningful conversation about moving through the gateway from a relatively happy human to an enlightened being. This spiritual guide challenged me and laid out key distinctions I'd not yet understood. The experience was a rebirth for me, magnifying the ease and grace in all areas of my life.

It's time to make unshakable inner peace your normal state. Imagine what's possible when you live within this space. Imagine what could happen if you were never triggered by others again. Imagine what you could achieve if you quieted your mind and took inspired action.

To support your transformation, I have created a course for you with practices and meditations to help clarify the process and embed this wisdom into every cell of your body. You can find that at UnshakableSeries.com. I also offer a contemplative question at the end of each chapter for you to hold with a curious mind or journal.

Unshakable Inner Peace is the first book of three in the *Unshakable Series*. You will soon experience why being receptive is the most significant state to be in as you enter the realm of the Divine. Being receptive goes far beyond getting good at accepting questionable compliments from Uncle Wayne at the family BBQ. A mental, emotional, physical, and energetic frequency opens you to unshakable certainty, where you are held by infinite support.

After you finish this book, you'll find more revelations in Book Two and Book Three. If you feel inspired, ask a friend or two to read this book and discuss its relevance in their lives. When you witness others in their confusion and realizations, and they see yours, an exponential power kicks in.

Spiritual awakening will affect every area of your personal and professional life. Are you ready to question everything you've been told about what creates and inspires awakening? Let's begin by acknowledging that we must first be willing to look like fools. I wish I could start the story by making myself look good, but that wouldn't be honest. I've been caught in all the ego traps known to man.

Let me tell you all about it.

CHAPTER ONE:
HEALING OLD WOUNDS

I opened an email with URGENT in the subject line.

> *"Is it still safe to come? The news headlines here in New*
> *Zealand report: Big Island Breaking Apart!*
> *Love,*
> *Monica"*

The Kilauea volcano erupted days before my husband Datta and I touched down on the Big Island of Hawaii. In the Spring of 2018, Kilauea gave us a demonstration of nature's power, with hundreds of homes destroyed. Fissures split the earth for lava to reveal its iridescent brilliance. As tourists and locals evacuated in droves, we made our way up the coast in our rental car.

Clients were slated to fly in from around the world for two retreats I was to lead. We had booked the Mauna Lani resort a year before without knowing a volcano could affect our safety. A volcanic eruption always leads to the expansion of an island. Was this a metaphor for human life as well? Could those who remain present to the explosions in their own life grow because of their courage to stay in the fire, versus numbing out and avoiding it?

I replied to Monica's email after we arrived, not knowing I was about to witness some of the most significant personal eruptions my clients had ever been through. Neither did I know that I wouldn't be spared, either.

"All are safe and well here, Monica. Where we are in
the northwest corner of the island, there's no sign of the
volcano or toxic ash. I look forward to seeing you soon.
Much love,
Rachael Jayne."

My Japanese students told me they felt Goddess Pele, the Hawaiian Goddess of volcanoes, had called them with her invitation. *Are you serious about transformation?* They answered unanimously, 'Hai!' Of all the cultures I've worked with, I have found the Japanese to take their personal development practices most seriously. They respect discipline and ritual and rarely get caught in the 'I already know that' trap many Westerners fall into. After teaching spiritual, psychological, and embodiment practices for more than fifteen years, I'd become cynical about spiritual seekers who acted as if they were further along on their path than they were. I don't care how much someone knows. I care how much someone lives what they know.

The beautiful entrance to the Mauna Lani resort underscored the dramatic timing of our arrival. We walked through the tall glass doors into an indoor courtyard that seemed to touch the sky. A circle of fifty-foot palm trees kissed the top balcony as live ukulele music wafted through the wispy leaves. We turned the corner to the registration desk and saw fresh pineapple juice and leis set out for us. The resort rested on a pristine sandy beach adorned with hammocks, sun lounges, and black lava rock. We had this sanctuary almost all to ourselves for eleven days.

We had been on the north shore of Oahu two weeks before, where international surf competitions are held. My soft body and Scottish–Irish skin were a giveaway that I was not there to surf.

I was there to write my next book.

An unexpectedly clear voice spoke to me through the writing process and gave me specific directions for my spiritual journey. As I left the writing retreat, something special started to form within me. I began to have mystical experiences and surges of extraordinary bliss. It was like someone had given me new eyes to see with and upgraded the level of pleasure I could enjoy.

I woke after my first night on the Big Island, sat in bed, and tucked my pillow behind my lower back to meditate. I felt a strange sensation, like something tugging on the back of my head, and noticed a quieter inner space than usual, with no mental chatter. Every morning that week, as I led my retreat on feminine presence, I was greeted with the same experience of peace, and my head was tugged backward by the same invisible force.

The second retreat I led on the Big Island was translated into Japanese. I loved being translated by Amrita. She was a good friend who had taught the *Art of Feminine Presence* training in Japan, and was masterful at conveying the nuances of my message. Translation slowed me down, however. It forced me to make every word clear. Speech became a meditation.

On the third day of this second retreat, I prepared to share my inner experience of this persistent presence that was forming in the core of my body. I looked around the concentric circles of Asian eyes and basked in the beauty of how different they were from my deep-set blue eyes. With marker in hand, I outlined a human form on the whiteboard and one word at the top – RECEIVE.

"We are a receiving channel," I declared. "We receive higher energy frequencies through our body's Vertical Core. When we become more receptive, our bio-energetic field strengthens and can take in and keep more of the higher frequencies it receives. The more we receive, the more energy will flow through us. The challenge is that high-frequency energy gets attracted to stuck energy because it tries to dissolve old resistance patterns. That's a great thing, but it's uncomfortable when we shine a light on something that isn't going well. It feels unnerving because the high-frequency energy awakens something that is an unconscious pattern you've tried to avoid. We have all created adaptive strategies to dodge around what we don't want to look at. If we dare to stay present with the discomfort in our body while higher frequency energy hits our resistance pattern, the contraction will eventually loosen, allowing that higher frequency energy to flood in and clear out old residue."

Earlier that week, I had explained this on a Zoom call with a group of clients, and one of them called the process 'hitting the *Oh, shit! Button.*' There was no better name for it. When energy and attention start to move toward something we've been trying to avoid, alarm bells ring, and the thought comes, *Oh, shit. . . What's going to happen if I go there? Let me stay in my comfort zone.*

I saw this play out every day of the retreat. An initial fear would arise when someone focused on something they had avoided. Sometimes it came with a visceral reaction like extreme coughing or nausea. Other times it was a deep emotional release of sadness or anger. After receiving this as a concept through my writing process a week before, I was now experiencing it in front of my eyes.

After lunch on the third day, my attention was drawn to Lao, a woman in her late thirties with long dark waves who sat across from me in our circle.

"I feel like it is your turn," I said.

She replied in polite Japanese, "I don't have anything to process myself, but I want to share something with you, Rachael Jayne."

"I would love to hear it."

She looked at Amrita, then back at me. "I want to tell Rachael Jayne I have been seeking enlightenment for many years. I have been to India to sit in temples with gurus. I have looked up to masters I've put on pedestals, making me feel small and unworthy. Now, I look at you today and what is happening to you and see that enlightenment is possible."

Enlightenment. As soon as I heard that word, my throat started closing. My body rejected her words. Tears filled my eyes.

Lao continued, "You are a wonderful teacher of love and compassion, and I now see that through your practices, I can experience what I've been searching for. It's wonderful to be with an enlightened spiritual teacher that is feminine. Most gurus are men."

My body resisted again, and my throat closed until I couldn't speak. I tried to loosen the constriction by stretching my neck from side to side, but it didn't help. It became hard to breathe. I looked down at the hotel carpet and knew I had a small window to make a fast decision; otherwise, the opportunity would be gone in seconds. The decision was to feel this resistance fully and go toward the constriction so I could heal this pattern of shutting something off at my throat. The other choice would be to try my best to pull myself together. After all, I was the facilitator of an international group that wanted to experience an advanced program in the *Art of Feminine Presence.* Was it my time to be my most vulnerable self in front of everyone?

The hand of the Divine was more potent than my rational mind. Before I knew it, I heard myself say, "I'm hitting some strong resistance. I need a moment."

Silence. Reverence. Amrita leaned over and whispered, "We are here for you, Rachael Jayne. We are here for you to feel this."

That loving gesture was enough to put me right into the mouth of the tiger. I stretched my mouth open and gasped for breath as best as possible. The constriction moved up my neck into the base of my head. I was reminded of the instructions I had given everyone else in their release process, to feel the constriction fully. To not tell a story about why it's there, or try to reason with it. I needed to bring presence to it, and not try to calm it down. I knew closing my mouth would calm it down. I kept my mouth open as my jaw wanted to clamp it shut.

"We're here for you, Rachael Jayne," Amrita repeated. "It's safe to feel it."

"Oh, God!" This exclamation, amplified by my microphone, ricocheted off the walls. This isn't going to look pretty, I thought to myself. I bent over and felt I was about to pass out.

Why such an intense reaction to a beautiful compliment from a young woman? On a cognitive level, I understood that constriction was about the fear of people's judgment. It was not safe to be called enlightened. I wanted a spiritual awakening, but now that someone saw it in me and shared it publicly, I was experiencing utter terror. There was no time to psychoanalyze this. I was bent over and in the throes of heaving and wailing, which I couldn't stop even if I tried. The sheer embarrassment did not match the energy coming up and out of my throat. There were sounds I'd never heard myself make before. It went on for fifteen minutes while everyone sat still. No one tried to fix or calm me down.

Finally, the eruption simmered down, and my sweaty body came to rest. There was no sound except the secondhand clock on the wall. I eventually leaned over to Amrita. "Please tell them we'll do a 30-minute break. I need to get on the floor and ground myself. I feel tender." She nodded and gave the instruction in Japanese.

As the group broke for afternoon tea, I looked for the darkest place in the room to lie down. Amrita approached my corner of the room and laid her cotton sarong over my body. Lao came over to kneel beside me. I couldn't speak her language, so we communicated through our eyes. She held my feet as I eventually covered my eyes with the sarong.

My mind could not fully comprehend those moments. What happened? What was it for? Why did I feel so expansive and peaceful after the intensity passed? In the days to follow, I felt even more profound stillness. No critical, doubting, anxious, comparing voice. No inner commenting on myself or others.

The fourteen days I spent in Hawaii writing and teaching had gifted me with the most profound awakening experiences I'd had up to that point. When I look back, the timing wasn't random. Something I did five months prior set this awakening in motion.

....

Contemplative Question:
What strategies do you use to avoid feeling emotion?

Access this chapter's guided practice in the *Unshakable Inner Peace* course at: UnshakableSeries.com

CHAPTER TWO:
IS ENLIGHTENMENT
POSSIBLE?

New Year's Day, five months earlier.

I stare out the living room window to the broad vista of snowcapped Colorado Rockies. What will my resolutions be? With a journal and pen, I write:

Weight training once a week
Shut down my computer by 9 pm
Meditate longer in the mornings

The next line surprises me:

I want to reach enlightenment this lifetime.

Huh? Where had that come from? I wasn't expecting such a boastful claim. Part of me greeted the thought with joyful curiosity, but the rest of me met it with a furrowed brow.

I've always had what I consider important and worthy goals. I was once given the gift of a burgundy mug with metallic gold letters that spelled out *Goal Digger*. I laughed when I opened that mug from its gift box and wondered if I was really that transparent. I had read enough about enlightenment to understand that it wasn't a goal to achieve. I believed it was a moment-to-moment state of experiencing your essential self instead of your separate ego self. I thought there would be no destination on my spiritual journey where my body or mind would never be irritated again. I knew the ego played a valuable role in keeping me alive and showed me the importance of creating boundaries. Even though I was already into a twenty-year relationship with meditation and spiritual practice, it was obvious to me I had not yet arrived in the place Eckhart Tolle talked about from his guru chair.

After I wrote "I want to reach enlightenment this lifetime" on that journal page, a lump formed in my throat, and the fear of judgment rose in me like a familiar enemy. I knew this was not something I could share with friends and family without receiving serious eye rolls or snarky comments. I was sure people would think, "Who does she think she is to even consider she's anywhere close to enlightenment?"

As an Australian, I've been schooled in the Tall Poppy Syndrome. When a poppy becomes too tall, it gets cut down to size, so all the poppies are even and orderly. The Brits are great at this, too. They can cut someone down with a vicious bite that might masquerade as friendly sarcasm. That kind of conversation lost its charm on me long ago, but not before leaving its scars. Too often, I'd interacted with someone who felt it was their responsibility to deflate my sense of confidence. I've been called arrogant or too full of myself more times than I can recall. I know I'm supposed to believe they're doing it for my own good, so my head won't swell too much. Like Pavlov's dog, this conditioned me to cringe when it was publicly noticed if I excelled at anything, and I didn't feel safe.

Being an Aussie female, I knew the importance of not shining too much or sharing lofty goals, so I attempted shrinking to fit in the way everyone around me did. To tell anyone I was ready to commit to enlightenment this lifetime would feel like placing my head in a guillotine and releasing the blade myself.

As I marinated in this new desire, I contemplated sharing it with the person I trusted and loved most. Being witnessed by my husband would strengthen my intention, but it also made me apprehensive. My husband loves me, and I care for his opinion. He's also a challenger. Datta has been on a spiritual path for almost five decades. He's led an ashram in Spain, traveled to India eight times on spiritual quests, and is a spiritual teacher in his own right. He's more knowledgeable about spiritual traditions and texts than I and has a healthy skepticism of many spiritual teachers.

State of the Union is what we call our Tuesday night discussions, where we talk about the state of our relationship and bring up things that we don't want to push under the carpet. I decided this would be where I would reveal my intention for enlightenment.

I hadn't been so nervous with him since our first week of dating. I leaned back into the sofa for comfort, felt the flames of the fireplace, tried to relax, yet the knot in my stomach feared his skepticism. My intention was like a baby chick that had only just hatched, and I felt protective of that fragile budding desire. It felt like one of the most vulnerable things I'd ever considered telling him. He knew I was committed to my spiritual work. However, upgrading from my usual rituals to a declaration that I intended to reach enlightenment this lifetime was another story.

My throat started to close over with the thought of sharing. This happened whenever I tried to share critical personal truths, so at half volume, I uttered, "I want to share a new intention with you."

"Okay," he said calmly, as he could see I was nervous, "I'd love to hear it."

"I've been sitting with this since New Year's Day," I started, "and I don't need you to do anything about this or help me with it, but you are my closest supporter, so I want you to know."

His blue eyes smiled with intrigue.

My breath seemed stuck, yet somehow or other I managed to get my words out. "I realize that even though spiritual growth has been my highest priority, I've believed it's impossible for me to experience enlightenment in this lifetime."

I paused, trying to read his expression, then leaped. "I have just set my intention to reach enlightenment this lifetime."

I tried to suck in another shallow breath in the awkward silence.

My husband's smile was still on his face, but I felt tension in the room.

"Wow, that's a big intention."

"Yep."

"Do you know it can take dozens of lifetimes for enlightenment to occur?"

There it was. Not the response I hoped for, but the one I expected. In defense, my voice hardened. "I know it takes a long time, but I'm not expecting or needing it soon. I feel this intention is next for me."

He nodded slowly. "Okay, but what do you mean by enlightenment?"

I couldn't figure out if there was now a smirk on his face or if my insecurity made that up. "I'm open to experiencing what that means."

"Many people try to be enlightened and even think they are . . . but they're not," he said with a bit of an edge to his voice.

"I agree," adding more edge to mine.

"How will you know when you are enlightened?"

"I don't know."

He sighed. "True enlightenment is no small thing. There are so many layers of the ego to get past."

I fell silent, feeling my frustration. I wanted to shout, "Can't you say, 'Wow, honey! I love that intention. Go for it!'" Instead, I asked, "Are you saying these things so I don't get my hopes up?"

"No. I'm just saying that most people will never be able to achieve what you want."

"I agree. Do you at least like and support my intention?"

"Yes, of course I do. But I think...."

At that point I tuned out his words. I brought my awareness back to my body, which felt tense and embarrassed. I felt he'd challenged me too fast. I wondered if he was concerned that I would get too pompous and think I was more enlightened than I was, which we'd seen a lot of in our line of work.

I knew Datta supported me on my spiritual path more than anyone. He's among the most sensitive, generous, and insightful people I've met. Was I reading too much into his reaction? I'd projected on him many times before. As I maneuvered the conversation off me, he shared his week and some of his New Year's intentions about health, spirituality, and his greatest passion, writing. I decided not to share more about this intention that flowered within me. I'm open to challenge, but this seed in me needed time to grow roots to weather a storm like the one that I felt just blew through.

Datta lifted himself from the couch and walked to the kitchen to fill his water bottle. I looked out the window at the same Rocky Mountains as when the thought arrived on New Year's Day. I reminded myself that this goal wasn't something I made up from my ego to try to feel significant or superior. I received the thought. I received this desire. It arrived from somewhere other than my mind.

Enlightenment. I'd heard at least a hundred definitions of it. Some intellectual, some mystical. Some confused me, and some aroused my heart. Many have called me an evolved soul, but even with my previous tastes of altered consciousness, there was something I did not yet comprehend about the mysterious promise of enlightenment.

To give you a sense of my inner landscape at the time, I would experience a solid inner peace around most people. My mind didn't have as much negative chatter as in the past, and I was almost always happy because I had learned to focus on gratitude and what was possible versus what wasn't. I had become good at being present with myself and others while under stress. But the moment I would feel anyone judging me, I lost stability. Certain types of people snapped me out of a compassionate space, especially those who were arrogant, critical, and insensitive. Every year fewer people upset me, but the list of people who still rattled my cage could fill a page. My comparing mind sometimes hijacked me when someone would share a big win and make me feel like something was missing within me. Occasionally, in tough conversations, I would want to scream because I was so angry my skin would crawl.

After my awkward declaration to Datta, I woke each day with curiosity about enlightenment and the complexity of what was required. I didn't want to learn about it in a book, in a religious text, from my husband, or a YouTuber. I wanted an intimate experience. I wanted to be consumed in its majesty. I would hold the sincere intention with all my heart each morning as I slipped into my meditation chair with our greyhound Dakota at my feet.

At the time, I didn't realize how much my focus and sincerity with this intention would speed the process up. When I thought about enlightenment, I thought of more ease in my day and mystical experiences appearing naturally. What unfolded didn't look so graceful. What waited around the corner for me was a huge lesson in humility.

....

Contemplative Question:
Do you believe living with unshakable inner peace is possible?

Access this chapter's guided practice in the *Unshakable Inner Peace* course at: UnshakableSeries.com

CHAPTER THREE: FEARING JUDGMENT

Five months later, in Hawaii, I entered the writing retreat room with a warm glow in my heart. The weather helped. I was on Oahu to write my third book, then lead some Big Island retreats. Being a landlocked Coloradoan, all my senses were in blissful expansion. The massive hotel windows framed an iconic view of palm trees and bronzed surfers riding giant waves to shore. The ocean's smell and my summer dress's satin finish softened my edges. The swing in my hips was always more pronounced when I visited one of the Hawaiian Islands.

I chose my seat near the front of the room, pulled out my thick spiral-bound notebook from my laptop bag, and laid two pens beside it in perfect vertical symmetry. I always start a book writing by hand. It allows my right brain to lead so I can connect with the soul of the book, rather than what my logical mind *thinks* it should be about.

Forty-four of our inner-circle clients were there with Datta and I to birth their books as well. After hugs and opening statements, it was time to begin. We were guided to take a deep breath and blow it out with solid force by our workshop leader, Tom. Another breath in and another breath out. The forty-six of us had created our wave as we breathed in and out together in rhythmic unison.

This is the life, I thought. I loved to write and didn't get a chance to focus on that craft as much as I wanted to. For the next four days, I would dedicate myself to this mysterious new book I was about to meet. I had no plan or outline for the book and was ready to receive it.

Pen to paper. Another deep breath in and out. My mind became still as I wrote across the top of the page…

Hawaii, May 2018.
I am ready to write my next book.

Along with the warm, salty breeze against my skin, I felt a palpable presence arrive in the space around me. I was not alone. I felt something or someone loving me, and I welled up with tears.

As I stared into space, I heard a clear voice speak to me. I could not make out if I knew whose voice it was, but it was as clear as if they were sitting next to me.

I watched my hand move the pen and transcribe what I heard.

> That's right. You're not alone. But the question is, are you willing to give up control and surrender to this writing process so I can help you with your mission to awaken? If you are eager, the conversation in this book will be the elevated conversation you've been asking for.

Conversation? I asked the voice by writing it on a new line.

> Don't concern yourself with how this book unfolds. Just tune into my voice. Can you hear my voice?

Yes. It's so clear. More precise than the thoughts in my head.

The battle inside your head will come to a natural end as you surrender to this conversation.

That sounds good.

I'm so proud of you, Rachael Jayne. You've been committed to your personal and spiritual development. Your self-reflection and self-observation are dialed in. You've gone through some dark tunnels and come out on the other side with more resilience. This book will guide others through their dark nights and into the light in more ways than you can imagine. It will lead you further into unconditional presence, and let you feel the unshakable peace that comes with that. Don't think about chapters, titles, or how to market this book. That will come later. Let us be together for a few days before you engage your strategic business brain.

Yikes! It's hard for me to surrender my strategic brain. I would at least like to know what this book is about before too long.

Trust me, the writing of this book will move your soul's purpose forward. Don't think about your marketing plan yet.

I'll try, but my mind can be stubborn. I'm a Triple Taurus, after all.

I won't hold that against you.

Cheeky.

> I like to have fun, which may sometimes be at your expense. Many guides and angels are gathering around you to help you write this book. They are coming toward you because you are an evolved one. A saint.

A saint? What the hell? I'm definitely not that.

> That word might jar you a little, since you were brought up Catholic. In that tradition, saints are the holiest of holies and have this title bestowed on them by others. But the true definition of the word saint is close to the Divine. A saint can surrender to the Divine and allow that connection to pour through them with their work on the earth. In that way, you are a saint.

Well, the first thing I'll do when I revise this book is remove the word 'saint.' I can't say that. It's way too arrogant.

> Please keep it in. I will point you toward specific terms for a reason. I will define them within the essence that they are intended.

Why is the word 'saint' important?

> Most people would have the same reaction as you. They are uncomfortable with the words saint, enlightened, or awakened. Part of what this book will do is to dispel the

myth that to become a saint or enlightened is only for a chosen few. For too long, religious, new age, and spiritual dogma have kept enlightenment only for the rock stars such as Jesus, Buddha, Mohammad, or the Dalai Lama. Eckhart Tolle might have slipped into this elite group with the help of Oprah.

You're funny!

It's time for you to go through this next gateway of awakening. This will be an elevated conversation because you are elevating yourself. All realizations are born from questions. This book will be the answer to your most important question.

I've heard that the quality of your life comes from the quality of your questions.

True. This book will focus on your most important question of all. Make sure you choose the right question, as you only get one.

What question is the most important one?

You decide that. What is the essential question you hold in your heart these days?

It seemed like a lot of pressure to come up with one poignant question if the whole book was to revolve around it. I took a deep breath and let out a quiet sigh. I already knew the burning question I wanted to ask. As I watched a man and a woman outside surfing by in an effortless communion with nature, I knew it was the right question. I scribbled it across the page.

> *Is it possible for me to reach enlightenment in this lifetime?*

Before I could form another thought, the voice inserted itself with an emphatic,

> Yes.

Really?

> Yes.

Are you sure?

> Yes.

Are you absolutely sure?

> This could get tiresome.

I'm sorry. I want to be sure I heard you correctly.

> You sound surprised by my answer.

I am. I wasn't expecting such a definitive answer. It doesn't feel like an easy thing to achieve.

> It's not easy, but it's available to you.

In this lifetime?

> Again, yes. Is that your one question?

That's the question that feels more significant than any other to me at this time.

> Good. That's your one question for this book. The answer is simple, and it is yes. Book done. That was easy.

Are you serious?

> Just kidding. I crack myself up sometimes. But you're still surprised at how easily I answered yes.

Kind of. On the one hand, I knew this to be true, as I have felt a constant pull toward spirituality my whole life. On the other hand, everything I've read or been told about enlightenment makes it sound like a mysterious, mystical experience that only one in a billion attains.

> I used specific words when I said, "it's not easy, but it's available to you." I used the word available, not attainable, for a reason. People often use the word attain or achieve when describing the process of enlightenment.

These are not great words to use as it activates the seeking mind, which is never satisfied and always thinks there's an end goal it needs to reach. The seeking mind is what dies during the awakening process. The word 'available' sparks a more accurate sentiment. What is available is always there for you. You just need to open the door and walk through.

I can't imagine it's as easy as opening a door and walking through.

That's why I'm here to help. We can peel back the layers of myths about enlightenment in this book. There is so much misunderstanding with the word enlightenment. It's like the word God. There are practically as many definitions for God as there are humans on earth. Together we can explore what enlightenment is—and what it's not—on your way to living in this stage of consciousness. It's not something you achieve. It's something to evolve into. You are moving in that direction. It's just a matter of time. Let's be with your question for a while so more can be revealed to you.

I paused to contemplate what I had already written in my notebook. I felt self-conscious. I sat down to write a book for my clients in The Awakened School community, and now I'm having this personal conversation that other people will read. I looked around the room at the others in their writing flow. *Who am I to think I can reach enlightenment in this lifetime? Who am I even to be* having *this conversation?* Before I could get further down my self-doubt rabbit hole, the voice forcefully interrupted.

Keep writing! Stop thinking!

What will others think of me when they read that I'm considering being able to evolve into enlightenment in this lifetime?

> Your journey has begun. I'll show you precisely what guards the doorway to enlightenment for you, Rachael Jayne. Let's start with a big one. You're afraid of what others will think of you.

Well, I have reason to be. I've been judged by others all my life. Just last week, someone emailed my team to criticize me. People who don't know me personally sometimes feel they have a right to dump their projections about me on to anyone who'll listen. It's not always easy to read these snarky comments that are not true. They probably share them with more people than just my team, and I have no control over that. It hurts.

> Well, boo-hoo. Join the party. Everyone else on this planet is constantly being judged as well. Your ego reacts and you try to control others' perceptions of you. The fight to control others stops you from constant inner peace. That's on you, not them.

I understand it's my ego, but knowing that doesn't make it easier not to react to their comments.

> It's hard not to pay attention to what others think of you, but as we converse, do your best to let fears about judgments

fall into the background. You'll never be able to receive this book if you think about people's potential reactions when they read this. No one can live a liberated life with constant concern about others' responses to their choices. On the journey towards enlightenment, all fear of judgment disappears naturally, on its own, without having to wrestle with it.

I can't imagine a day when the fear of judgment wouldn't affect me.

Giving up what others think is hard for you, yet it will eventually happen.

It sure is hard. *What will people think when they read this conversation?* That thought won't stop. It's on an endless loop. How can I let that concern go?

It's okay that those thoughts are present. Most thoughts come from past conditioning. Don't try to get rid of them. Just notice them. Notice how they find their way onto the blank screen of your mind without your permission. Don't let your mind hijack you from being present in the conversation we'll have together. You will write the words you hear me say, and then you can have your response and ask me the next question. If you notice your mind is concerned about what others will think, let those thoughts find their way to the background of your awareness, not front and center. Tune your focus in a way that allows your fearful thoughts to become like the background music at a coffee shop or the low-level chatter of the people in the next room. Can you hear the voices in the next room?

Yes. There must be around thirty people in there. I can't make out what the main presenter is saying, though.

They're having a good time, aren't they?

They are. I suspect it's an annual function of some sort. I perceive smiles from some and seriousness from others but can't make out the words.

Notice what it's like to hear sounds from another room, and at the same time, remain aware that these distant voices are not your own.

I can do that. It feels nice. It feels like I can have my space and feel my presence no matter what happens. I guess no one can interrupt our conversation unless I let them.

Exactly. Do this anytime you have thoughts about potential judgments. Tune your focus so they are in the background. You can invite those thoughts to wait in the next room. Don't banish or fight them, but instead say, "Would it be okay if you hung out in the other room for a while if I promise to come and get you later?"

It feels good in my body when I contemplate that. It relaxes my system. My negative thoughts and feelings won't suffocate me if I can invite them to hang out in the next room.

> I'm glad you already feel how your body responds to what I say, as your body is part of the mechanism that will tell you when you're enlightened.

There it is again. Within a split second of hearing the word enlightened, my mind revolts with, *what will people think of me when they hear this arrogant conversation?*

> First of all, you didn't think that thought. The thought arose within your awareness. Thoughts arise because of past experience. You didn't choose to have that thought, did you?

No, I didn't. It just showed up without being asked.

> Stop and take a moment to ask the part of you that worries about judgments, "Are you willing to hang out in the other room for a while?"

I asked without attachment and it feels like it's leaving the room, as though something heavy and annoying just left. I'm surprised at how spacious I feel so soon after a simple invitation to hang out in the next room. So, where were we?

> You can leave your mind at the door of any room you walk into. The mind loves to be in control, so if you ask

its permission directly, it will grant you what you ask for. Giving consent makes it feel like it's in control.

I'll be sure to use this technique again.

Good, you'll need it.

Inviting the mind to take a back seat is like one of the *Art of Feminine Presence* practices I teach. After working with those practices, many clients tell me this work is a piece that's been missing in their lives.

That's because you work with the different areas of human and spiritual development that need to come together for inner peace to be a consistent experience. However, as we continue our conversation, you will see that you still miss pieces in your understanding that are not in your body of work to the level needed for spiritual realization.

Really?

Yes, really.

I'm intrigued.

Good. Before we get to what's missing and how to fill in the gaps for greater understanding, let's talk about the most important of all forty-four practices that you teach in the *Art of Feminine Presence* and *Art of Masculine Presence* when it comes to spiritual awakening.

Contemplative Question:
Where do thoughts originate?

Access this chapter's guided practice in the *Unshakable Inner Peace* course at: UnshakableSeries.com

CHAPTER FOUR:
OPEN TO RECEIVE

This might shock you, but the essential practice that opens the gateway to spiritual awakening is the one you consider least important.

What?

You forget to teach it at least a third of the time you lead a training session. If you remember you missed it, you squeeze it in at the end for a few minutes or have one of your team teach it on a Zoom call later. Sometimes you consciously skip it. You think, "This practice is boring and less essential than the others," but you're wrong.

My mind scrolls through the list of practices I'd been teaching for the past decade.

It would be best if you put this practice in the first session of the first day. Everything builds from this fundamental practice. To forget this practice proves how off-track you are with comprehending how enlightenment unfolds.

You're killing me here. Which practice?

Drum roll, please. . . .You call it Receptive Body.

My goodness. Really?

Yes, really. It's also the practice most important for the conversation we'll have over the next few days. You'll receive my voice. You'll receive insights. It makes sense to practice being more open to receiving.

I can understand how being receptive helps me receive your message, as it relaxes my system and stops the mind from jumping in so quickly. However, I'm surprised that you consider it the most important practice for spiritual awakening.

You just gave yourself a clue. It will relax the system without the mind jumping in so quickly.

Okay, that makes sense.

Let's do the practice together to sense what happens. This will let you gather more ideas about why this is such a fundamental practice.

You mean right here in the writing retreat room?

Yes, I'll guide you. As your fingers hold your pen, let your body fall into the receptive experience.

Okay.

> The way you hold your body affects how receptive you are. The way you breathe affects how receptive you are. The way you talk and the way you listen affect how receptive you are. Does your current posture and breath create receptivity right now?

I think so. I could lengthen my spine and breathe deeper.

> Do that now. Create more spaciousness in the internal space of your body.

It feels good to imagine more space between each vertebra. It makes me feel more open to receiving.

> Now bring your attention to your hands. Notice how your hands feel when they are in giving mode. Imagine they must give energy to someone.

When the energy of my hands is in giving mode, I sense less of the inner energetic presence that runs through my hands. I feel less embodied in my hands. I can't help but have my attention on what I'm giving *to* rather than on my hands.

> Now, imagine opening your hands to receive the love and abundance that wants to flow to you. Put your hands in receptive mode and tell me what you experience.

I feel a pleasurable sensation of buzzing in my hands. I find it easy to enjoy being inside my hands. My awareness goes inward, which seems to settle my mind. It all feels good.

> Now bring your attention to your heart. Notice how your heart feels when it's in giving mode. Imagine your heart is giving energy to someone.

It's hard to feel the glow in my heart that I'm used to feeling. It's as if my focus gets pulled out of my heart and onto something in front of me. Like with my hands, I feel less inner energetic presence, and less embodied.

> Now, imagine opening your heart to receive the love and abundance that wants to flow to you. Put your heart in the receptive mode and tell me what you experience.

I need to pull my attention back into the center of my chest to make my heart receptive. As I come back into my body, I can feel the glow of my heart. I remember your words, *receive the love and abundance that wants to flow to you.* I relax and open up even more. A smile comes to my face and my joy meter rises. It feels great. I could stay here all day.

> Now bring your attention to your whole body at the same time. Notice how your body feels when it's in giving mode. Imagine your body is giving energy to someone.

The pleasure in my body decreases. My attention gets pulled forward and out of the core of my body. I'm not aware of my energy centers. I feel tighter somehow.

> Now, imagine opening your whole body to receive the love and abundance that wants to flow to you. Put your entire body in receptive mode and tell me what you experience.

I imagine all my cells open to drink in the sun on this perfect Hawaiian day. The corners of my mouth spontaneously curl up. I feel relaxed again. The longer I stay in this receptive space, the more I feel like I'm glowing.

> You *are* glowing. When you are in the receiving mode, your bio-energetic field gets stronger.

Is this what they mean when people say, 'Your vibration or frequency rises?"

> Yes. When you are receptive, your frequency rises. You are lighter. When you feel you must give your energy away, it decreases.

But sometimes giving to someone else feels pleasurable.

> If you were giving to someone, what would you do to make yourself as present and joyful as you are right now, as you receive?

When I imagine giving my energy to someone I love, at the same time receiving the love and abundance that wants to flow through me, I immediately feel centered in my body. It feels good.

That's right. You never need to only give and forget yourself. Certain people only slide into the receptive experience when they give in an enjoyable way. Giving brings them intimately into the now experience, which pulls them into receptivity. All action can and should be in the receiving mode if awakening is the outcome you want.

I love the sound of that, and can relate to it as a musician. When I perform, the way I get into the zone is to receive the moment. I receive the band, I receive the audience, and I receive the way my voice wants to interpret the melody. I'm not always in that space in everyday life, but it's magical when I slip into that field of being. There's no self-consciousness. There's no performer consciousness of trying too hard. There's only presence.

Let's get back to your inquiry. How could Receptive Body be the fundamental practice of your work so far regarding enlightenment and living in a more expanded dimension of awareness? Given your experience toggling back and forth between giving and receiving, why do you think being receptive is essential?

I think there are various reasons. When I'm receptive, I am spacious and open. The body tells the brain that there is no need to defend itself. When I'm receptive, I realize there is so much beyond myself that I can receive. The focus comes off my small self and onto receiving infinite love and abundance. When my body relaxes, my mind relaxes and stops its automatic fixations on certain thought patterns. I feel as though I'm connected to the divine when I am in a receptive space. There's no object to focus on, and instead focus on experience.

> When you're receptive, you experience the moment versus being in your head. All these things you mention are bridges to the enlightenment experience you seek. If your stage of consciousness currently is on Island A and the stage of consciousness called enlightenment or sometimes called 'The end of seeking' is on Island B, the state of receptivity is the bridge. To make this journey, you must be open to receive.

Are there other ways I can practice being in a receptive space?

> Receive through others. People want to connect and love. Allow yourself to feel their love for you. Allow them to serve you.

I thought I was pretty good at letting people love and support me.

> Maybe so, but there are still edges for you to work on. What happened when you showed up at the San Francisco hotel a few weeks ago when your back was sore?

I was a silly girl that night. It was late after a big day of travel on my own from Colorado. My back hurt from carrying my luggage. On the drive to the hotel, I envisioned asking for help with my bags so I wouldn't do myself any more damage. However, when I arrived, I didn't want to embarrass myself by having to ask for help.

So you paid the physical price.

I did.

As you lighten your frequency, people will want to give you more support. Stretch into that. Receive whatever someone is easily and joyfully willing to give. Don't feel like you must take from others or fight for anything. There is no reason for that. In the experience of enlightenment, you will feel as if everything is being given to you, and it is.

That sounds beautiful.

It is. Every piece of exceptional artwork was received by the artist. Every great song was received by the writer. Every solution to a new problem was received first, then strategies emerged from that idea. Every great insight from a scientist was first received and then built upon. Some call it intuition. Einstein received insights while conducting his thought experiments, which deeply impacted his work on general relativity. He received images relevant to his work. The insights from those images were also received. They were received because his consciousness was pointed toward understanding more about general relativity, and his mind was open to receive.

He had to use his human and scientific skills to refine his hypothesis, prove It, and make it applicable to human reality—but first, he received.

It's the same process as writing a book. You are in a

receptive mode right now, but you still need to refine and structure the words so it's a cohesive read. You'll need to edit and proofread it before it's ready for human consumption. A painter still must add the finishing touches. A project manager who receives a great solution to a problem must still instruct their team. A teacher who has a great idea they want to express still needs to use their communication skills to articulate the concept clearly.

I think I see what you mean.

A body that experiences high-frequency love, power, and intuition receives that experience. A body that no longer needs to guard against anything receives that experience. The body doesn't make enlightenment happen. The body doesn't give and give until someday it's enlightened. It *receives* the experience of enlightenment.

How does it receive enlightenment?

The body doesn't receive enlightenment. The body can receive the experience of enlightenment.

What?

Stick with me. If this were easy for your mind to comprehend, it would have already done so. The body is your Earth Suit—like a space suit you would need to wear if you traveled to Mars. It's not you. Your body is not what gets enlightened hence I said the body doesn't receive enlightenment. The body doesn't get the gold star when enlightenment happens. However, it will *experience* enlightenment because perception occurs through the body. When you know with certainty who you are, and the resistance to that knowing fades, you will experience life through your physical senses in an infinitely expansive way. Enlightenment isn't intellectual knowledge of who or what you are. It's when your essential self recognizes itself through your human experience. When that shift occurs, you perceive everything as divine and feel like you have new eyes.

I will probably need to read what you just said multiple times before I get it.

No amount of re-reading will help you get it. You must experience it. That is why I will continue to guide you through experiences as we write this book together. Let's start with the mind and how it operates when experiencing expanded dimensions of consciousness.

Contemplative Question:
What does being receptive mean to me?

Access this chapter's guided practice in the *Unshakable Inner Peace* course at: UnshakableSeries.com

CHAPTER FIVE:
MY MIND IS NOT THE
ENEMY

You don't need to eliminate or ignore the mind to live with unshakable inner peace. You will never be rid of the mind, nor would you want to. It accomplishes a lot. Instead, you must perceive the mind as something you are aware of rather than believing you *are* the mind. Enlightenment is about living as the awareness that is aware of the awareness, that is aware of your mind.

That's a bit confusing.

Let me put it a slightly different way. Say this slowly to yourself three times: "I am the awareness that is aware of the observer that is aware of my thoughts, body, and emotions."

I pause and whisper it three times, as instructed, but don't feel as though the phrase sinks in.

When you speak that sentence, it's important to note that that statement has three dimensions of awareness. Those are:

1. The thoughts, body, and emotions you are aware of.
2. The observer who is aware of the body, mind, and emotions and comments on them.
3. That which is aware of the observer and all it observes.

For most people, the first dimension is easy to understand. We all know we have thoughts, a body, and emotions. Some people are aware of the second dimension. They know they have a self-reflective process they might call the 'observer' or 'witness' because they are aware that they comment on their thoughts, body, and emotions when they become aware of them. It's the distinction between the second and the third dimension where people get stuck.

When you say, "I am the awareness," in the sentence above, that refers to the third dimension of awareness, the fundamental essence of your self. You are aware. Are you not?

I believe so.

Everything you experience springs from your fundamental essence, which for now, we'll call awareness. The second dimension of awareness in this sentence is the self-reflective observer. It observes the body, thoughts, and emotions and makes comments like, "My hip is tight. I should have stretched this morning," or "I notice I'm triggered by what that person said." Are you aware of this observer who comments on your thoughts, feelings, and actions?

Yes, I am.

This is because you've spent much time and practice becoming more self-aware. Some people can't step back and observe that someone has triggered them. They are so triggered they blame the person for their upset. Do you notice that another dimension of awareness is aware of the commenting witness? Isn't it true that you are aware of the commenting observer?

Now that you've pointed it out to me, yes.

Is it true that you are aware you are aware?

I guess so.

That's the third dimension of awareness.

I think I get it, but it feels somewhat cerebral to me.

Right. Knowing this intellectually doesn't mean you experience it. When you *experience* this third dimension of awareness, the mind can't fixate on thoughts and feelings because this dimension of awareness doesn't comment on thoughts and feelings. In other words, it is not attached to thoughts and feelings, so they move through one's experience organically while your awareness is quiet and non-judgmental. It's the commenting observer (the second dimension) that makes your thoughts and feelings stick around and often causes suffering because it usually says something in judgment like, "This is bad," "this is scary," or "you didn't do it right." The commenter usually creates resistance toward what it is aware of. Your spiritual awakening expands to a new stage of consciousness when you live in the dimension of non-commenting awareness versus the dimension that is observing everything you're thinking and feeling but has an opinion on everything. This non-commenting awareness will soon become the primary way you perceive yourself. You won't experience yourself as the self-aware commentator. You'll see that it is a lower dimension of perception. So far in your awakening journey, you're missing immersing yourself in this third dimension. Even when you meditate and have spiritual practice time, you are primarily focused on being more self-aware, which is lovely. Then you end one step too early. You need more practice on resting as the awareness that is aware that you have a self-aware witness that comments.

Let me see if I have this. I see long-stemmed flowers in a tall cylinder vase at the front of the room. That's the first dimension of awareness you're pointing me toward— objects I'm aware of.

Yes.

I am aware of my mind that comments on the flowers. I like how they look because of their gorgeous royal purple and yellow blooms. The conscious observer who comments on the objects of my awareness is the second dimension of awareness. If I pause and ask myself the question, Am I aware that I am aware of the flowers and commenting on them? I would answer yes.

You got it.

I could also relate this to what I think. I have the thought; *I don't know if I want anyone to read this book.* That thought is something I'm aware of. Then, there is awareness of the thought. If I like the thought, it just drifts on organically. If I don't like the thought, the commenter starts in and creates resistance, and the thought sticks around and starts spinning.

> Good observation. The commenter creates the suffering, not the initial thought or feeling.

Then if I pause and ask myself if I'm aware that I am aware of that doubtful thought about this book? The answer is yes. I know that a self-reflective part of my mind observes and comments on that thought. It also starts to comment on why I'm silly to have that thought and to get over myself. It likes to comment on a lot of things.

I can relate this to hearing the waves outside this room. There is the sound, there is the awareness of the sound, and I am aware of the awareness of the sound. I could relate this to touching the smoothness of my ballpoint pen. There is the sensation, the awareness of the sensation, and I am aware of the awareness of the sensation.

> That's right. To shift attention from thoughts, feelings, and sensations to the commenting observer who can be aware of these thoughts, feelings, and sensations is wonderful. This is a psychological process of maturity on the path of awakening. The self-reflective process is vital because we cannot remain in the dimension where we believe we are our thoughts, body, and emotions.

Just don't stop there! Your next frontier is to continue to shift your attention from perceiving yourself as the self-aware commenter to perceiving that you are what is aware of this commenter. Once that non-commenting dimension of awareness has stabilized through your eyes and ears, you will be at ease no matter what happens around you. Why? Because this dimension never adds any resistance to anything. It doesn't comment. It's quiet.

Does it make sense now when I say you don't have to quiet the mind? You turn your focus to another dimension of perception that will already and forever be quiet.

I sense the difference between trying to be non-resistant and quiet my mind and shifting into this third dimension which is non-resistant at its core. It doesn't have to try to be non-resistant or still. It is.

That's right. This non-commenting dimension of awareness doesn't have to become more compassionate, unconditional, and non-judgmental; it is the *essence* of unconditional. When you shift your attention to this third dimension of awareness, your mind becomes the servant to this Essential Self rather than something with an opinion on everything.

That would be lovely.

There are many peaceful days ahead for you. For now, receive my voice, record it on the page, and we can dissect whatever doesn't make sense, so that it makes sense in your actual experience.

Thanks. Practical applications are what I want. I want to know how to transition from a relatively happy human to a fully awakened being.

> First, it's adorable that you use the words 'fully awakened being' when you don't know what that even means. Let's make it practical for you.
>
> To transition from a relatively happy human to an experience of consistent inner peace, how you focus attention must be agile enough to quickly move between these different dimensions of awareness. Multiple times a day, notice that you can perceive what happens from other dimensions of awareness. Take time to pause to ask, Who or what is viewing this situation? Or, who or what is seeing with my eyes? You only have one set of physical eyes, yet you can see from many dimensions. Everyone has this ability, no matter how self-aware they are. Being able to see within different dimensions is not just a superpower kept for the chosen few. The dimension you see within is determined by where your focus of attention is at any given moment. Enlightenment is consistently seeing from a particular dimension that we can call unconditioned awareness. This awareness doesn't judge or comment and puts no conditions on how you or life should be. Does that make sense?

Yes. I think I just had a significant a-ha moment. This unconditioned awareness is different from the commenting mind. I can see how my commenting mind tries to train me not to judge, not to comment on what is good or bad, and wants to teach me to be more peaceful.

Fantastic! That's a big a-ha indeed. No amount of training to be a perfect human being will drop you into unconditioned awareness and, in turn, unshakable inner peace. Trying to train the ego to be ego-less is ridiculous.

My mind is trying hard to understand what you just said, but it feels scrambled.

It's okay to let the mind be scrambled. It will never fully understand this topic because the only way to understand it is to be in the unconditional dimension of awareness. Self-awareness is a conditional dimension of awareness. It has been conditioned to comment on and judge what it sees and feels.

Okay, I'll let it be confusing.

Let's walk through the dimensions one more time, from a different angle, so it sinks in beyond the mind.

Yes, please.

When your ego-mind sees through your physical earth-suit eyes, it sees everything as separate from everything else. It immediately puts conditions on things, like they should do it this way, I should do it that way. This is because the ego is a protective mechanism that keeps the body and image safe. The ego mind thinks if you're not liked, you're not safe. If you don't get your needs met, you're not safe. If you're not seen as significant, you're not safe, and so on.

When the self-aware witness sees through your physical eyes, you can observe what is happening from a more detached vantage point. Its commentary sounds much wiser than the unedited thoughts in your head. However, it's still conditional awareness because it says things like, *you shouldn't think that way,* or *you should have said something when you saw that happen.* You can train the self-aware witness to step back and see how your mind works and how your knee-jerk reactions occur, making it easier to see you are more than thoughts, feelings, and sensations. This move from believing you are your thoughts to thinking you are the self-aware one looking at your thoughts is a giant leap for humanity, but it's not going far enough if you want to know and embody your peaceful essential nature.

What are examples of other comments a self-aware witness might make? Name a few.

- I feel anxious and overwhelmed and don't want to feel this way.
- I thought I had released an old pattern, but it still affects me.
- If I practice this behavior more, I could improve myself.
- That person is being a moron, but I won't let them disturb my peace.

You've brought up excellent examples here. Look back at what you just wrote and notice how the comments are conditional.

The first comment, "I feel anxious and overwhelmed and don't want to feel this way," puts a condition on unwanted feelings. The second comment, "I thought I had released that old pattern, but I can still feel it," puts the condition on the pattern, saying it shouldn't happen. The third comment, "If I do this behavior more, I could improve myself," puts a condition on the action. You should continually improve.

With the fourth comment, "That person is being a moron, but I won't let them disturb my peace," obviously, I'm judging the person, and there is a condition on how I should react.

> Very astute, particularly the last one. In the spiritual awakening journey, you don't make yourself peaceful. You unwind the contractions of your body-mind until you experience peace as your natural, unconditioned state.

In my workshops, I call that attempt 'pseudo harmony.' It's when people try to do something to become peaceful, like numbing out with a substance, reading romance novels, meditating, or trying to calm themselves down, so they don't look irritated or don't react. But it's only short-lived. It's not true unshakable peace, which I now understand comes from perceiving the world from another dimension of awareness.

> Most spiritual seekers think that if they get this self-aware part of them strong enough or find ways to calm themselves, it will lead to enlightenment because this leads them to not be identified with their ego.

I don't blame them. That's what I've heard from many teachers.

> That may be what you think you heard, but it's only one step. When you get some distance between your thoughts and the awareness of your thoughts, that is a tremendous psychological step supporting the spiritual awakening process. Still, as I keep repeating, it doesn't stop there. There is another set of eyes behind this self-aware observer. You've said you want me to make this practical, so answer this: Are you aware of the self-aware observer that notices and comments?

Yes, I am.

> Then see with that set of eyes right now. Sense yourself as the awareness that sees the observer who comments. These eyes are sensed when you are further back in your head. Take a moment to pause and rest your awareness behind your human eyes. Don't feel you need to look out through the front of your eyes. Look inward to the center of your head.

That feels relaxing.

> Now ask yourself again if you're aware of the self-aware observer that comments on what it observes.

I believe I am.

That is the third set of eyes.

I see.

You do see. You see with three sets of eyes. What do you notice about the third set of eyes?

They just observe. They don't comment or judge. There's no noise.

That's right. This is God looking through your eyes.

That's a big statement.

I know. God is unconditional. God doesn't comment or have any judgment. God doesn't want anything from you—or anyone else.
When you hear comments on what you witness, it's a sign you are in a more contracted dimension of seeing, other than the Infinite Presence that many call God, Source, or the Divine. Suppose God is not the word that resonates, given too many warped definitions placed on that word over time. In that case, you can use I see with the eyes of the Universe, I'm seeing with the eyes of my spiritual essence, or I'm seeing with the eyes of the Divine. Choose one that feels good to you.

I shifted my gaze to see with these third-level Universal eyes, and something remarkable happened. I just slipped into an altered state.

I'm not surprised, though while it is an altered state to what almost everyone lives in, it is your natural, essential state. This is the dimension of being I want you to become used to. These are the eyes to condition yourself to see with. This dimension of seeing will become standard with practice.

Everything is quiet in this place.

What else are you experiencing?

I feel further back in my head. It's as though a weight in the back of my head pulls me into the back half of my head. When I allow this pull to happen, I feel my energy field get brighter. I have a more intimate sense of my energy field. Thoughts are gone except the ones I need to stay present with for the writing experience. The weight in the back of my head is quite interesting.

You can only see with God's eyes through the central channel of your body. Looking through the center of your skull allows you to see from this dimension. When your attention is too far forward in your eyes, you see with your ego dimension, which gives you the sense that everything is separate from everything else. These eyes cannot see the interconnectivity of the Universe.

In a few minutes, the ego mind will try to take credit for your altered, blissful state. It will probably sound like, *wow, I am seeing through God's eyes.* But that would be inaccurate. There is no ego-mind looking. It is Infinite

Presence looking. It is pure unconditioned awareness looking through a body-mind instrument.

I hear that declaration from my ego mind already. It's helpful to know that the ego mind senses itself as a separate person. What do I do about the separate self that wants to claim victory for being so awesome?

> Let it do its thing but see right through it. Are you aware of the separate self's thoughts?

I believe so.

> That is the self-aware observer, watching from another dimension. Then, move back in your skull and ask: Am I aware of that observer?

Yes, I am.

> Good. Rest in that essential awareness. Be that unconditional awareness that doesn't comment or judge.

I'm going to take a few deep breaths and be still in that for a moment.

> Take your time.

As I rest in this place, a situation that happened a few years ago is strongly coming to my attention.

It's coming to you for a reason. When you are in this dimension of awareness, you will start to receive more because you are not in a contracted state. You'll receive images, metaphors, a-ha moments, dreams, and memories from the past that will support you to remain in this dimension. If they come when in the dimension of this Divine presence, they are signs and signals. What comes to mind?

It's a crazy story about a fuchsia tissue box, a black Porsche, a bear, and a pack of playing cards.

Ah yes. That was one powerful day.

....

Contemplative Question:
Who or what is looking out through my eyes?

Access this chapter's guided practice in the *Unshakable Inner Peace* course at: UnshakableSeries.com

CHAPTER SIX:
ECSTATIC INSIGHT

After watching a YouTube video on manifestation, I decided to play the game that was being described. The game was to choose four things I intended to see over the next few days and remain uplifted until I saw them. From what I'd been told, the game was originally created to experience through focus, joy, and non-attachment, we can draw things to us. Being unattached to seeing any of the chosen items is important because attachment adds resistance. I wanted to strengthen my trust in how I can consciously manifest what I put my attention on.

I took a moment to clear my mind, and the first four things that came to my awareness were:

1. A fuchsia tissue box
2. A black Porsche
3. A bear
4. A pack of playing cards.

I started the game one weekend when Datta was away on a work trip. I cherish alone time and didn't want to leave the house. However, I'd run out of toilet paper and had already started scavenging tissues from boxes scattered around the house. By Monday morning, I had three tissues left, and it was time for action.

Walking to the mailbox to get mail I had not wanted to leave the house for, I saw a tissue box that had blown into the middle of my front yard. At first, I wondered why a tissue box would be in the middle of our manicured lawn, and then it hit me… my game! It had fuchsia flowers printed on the sides, was more than half full, and was in my front yard! Given my urgent need for soft tissue, I record this as a better manifestation than imagined. The most useful of toiletries literally dropped fifteen feet in front of my doorstep, with fuchsia pink flowers, no less.

I had forgotten about the other three items in my game until I drove up the town's main drag to drop Dakota off at the local kennel. *I should look around for a black Porsche,* I thought. Within minutes I stopped at traffic lights, looked to my left, and a black Porsche convertible was sitting in the parking lot, bringing me profound joy.

Later that day, on the way to the airport, I told my driver what had happened with my manifesting game. She was particularly struck by the tissues in the front yard and by my exuberance. I was in an altered state from my usual way of being because I was extraordinarily open and happy.

"I think I might see a bear at the airport in one of those cheesy Colorado memorabilia stores," I stated.

"I wouldn't be surprised," she replied. "There are a lot of Colorado tourist shops in the concourses, and I'm sure there is a bear in there."

I hopped out of the car, checked my bag with the airline, and with boarding pass in hand, walked toward the escalators that led to the security gates. I put a slight smile on my face to purposely uplift my heart, and I repeated to myself in an unattached way, *where's my bear?*

My eyes were immediately drawn over to the Panda Express Eatery on the second floor, but there were no stalls of stuffed bears for sale.

I looked down at both ends of the terminal for a bear on a sign or T-shirt, but my eyes were drawn back to the Panda Express sign. It was as if my eyes had a mind of their own. I would look away to peer into other stores, but my head would return to Panda Express without my desire. It finally struck - a panda is a bear! My heart exploded with joy again.

How did this happen? I asked myself. What made my eyes move to land on the Panda Express sign when it was clear I didn't consciously choose to move my eyes? I was trying to look somewhere else. It didn't even occur to me that a panda was a bear until a minute later.

I soared down the escalator unable to stop the giggles. As I got to the TSA entrance, I heard an inner voice say to go into the store to the left and ask if they had a pack of cards. I did, and they did! Four out of four. My heart was beyond light while going through TSA. Not the usual place for an awakening moment.

The question I was with for days was, *what turned my eyes to see the Panda Express sign?* It felt like something other than me. Something that was inside me turned my eyes. Can you shed any light on this?

Your investigation into the dimensions of awareness is why this memory arose for you. What turned your head was the Infinite seeing through your eyes. It wasn't your ego mind trying to figure out where the bear might be. It was your Universal eyes. In other words, the divine interconnectivity of all things flowed through your body, which moved your body to look at the Panda Express sign.

You were already in a highly receptive state from the morning's sightings when Infinite Knowing turned your eyes that final time to make sure you saw the Panda

Express sign. That is what it feels like to have the energy of unconditioned awareness and presence course through every energy center and move you in perfect concert with the Universe.

It was one of the most powerful experiences of my spiritual life. But it has remained a mystery until now as to how that could have happened.

Your body was familiar with ecstatic states because you'd been practicing the *Art of Feminine Presence* for so long. You had trained your body to be more receptive, but because of everything that had unfolded that morning, your receptive channel was wildly more open than usual. All energy centers were open to receive impulses from the Infinite rather than impulses from your separate self. You already knew you could receive an idea or solution that helps manifest something you want. At the airport, you had the experience of how your physical form can receive the answer and how the physical form can move your body before your ego knows what's happening. This awakening journey is fundamentally about increasing receptivity.

Receptivity to what?

To the Divine. To the interconnectivity of everything experienced as Infinite love, power, and knowing. You have called it the Divine Matrix before. It's a great term to describe something indescribable.

What if the power and pleasure of this expanded place overwhelms me or others?

> I understand why you would have that point of view. Your energy is immense, becoming increasingly transparent by the day. However, moving into these expanded states will actually overwhelm people less.

Really? How so?

> Divine power is soft, peaceful, and inviting. When someone fears being "too much for people," it's their ego speaking. When someone pushes people away with big energy, it's not Divine power.

Isn't it a matter of someone not containing their life force, which ends up in other people's personal space and makes them uncomfortable?

> That is true in some cases. However, when someone moves into the Infinite dimension of the Divine, their energy gets more potent and contained in their core. It's lovely to be around, not intimidating.

I'd love an in-depth conversation about the energetics of enlightenment that you point to here, but I don't want to rush it. Can we come back to this topic later?

> For sure. Let's go back to the practice of recognizing what eyes you see with. Take a few minutes several times a day

to see only with the eyes of the Infinite but to see with the eyes of your separate self. Toggle back and forth between these two sets of eyes by first feeling more aware of the central vertical channel that runs through your body and your head, and then pay attention to what's in front of your eyes. You'll perceive the world differently in seconds.

I'd like to do that right now.

Take your time.

When I rest my awareness in the center of my head, my experience of the room is one seamlessly connected space. When my awareness is in the front of my head, I notice more of the separate objects in the room.

That's right. Another name for your Infinite eyes could be your Interconnectivity eyes, which see everything as part of one whole versus the separate self-eyes, which see everything as disconnected but in the same room.

When I look out from the center point of my head, I hear no comments from my mind about the room, and I feel a sense of ease.

The experience of no fear results from this way of perceiving the world—only unconditional viewing.

Looking out through my physical eyes, I notice judgment about each object I look at. Those eyes want to name the thing and then judge it as good or bad, pretty, ugly, practical or not. I start to feel a little anxious.

I could also ask myself, what ears am I listening with? The ears of presence and non-attachment or the ears that hear limitations, judgments, or conclusions of what it thinks is going on?

> That would be a great practice too. Be aware of the central vertical channel when you listen so you can listen with ears of Interconnectivity.

I will. I can feel how important attention within the vertical core is. It's funny because I've been teaching it in my programs to help people strengthen and contain their energy. Still, I don't understand how it can take us to a different dimension, and support spiritual awakening.

> How do you define the vertical core?

I would say it's an energetic column that runs vertically through the body and connects all the major energy centers along the spine. It's shown on many qi-gong or yoga diagrams where you can see the chakra system in vertical alignment. I perceive the vertical energy channel several feet above my head and several feet under the earth beneath me. It feels peaceful to feel this channel and to be in the center of my head, to rest in the center of my chest, and to spend time in the center of my belly.

> Not everyone feels the peace you describe when they contact the core of their body. Instead, they experience their pain body, which is unconscious resistance built up

from not being present. Being embodied and aware of your vertical core has a domino effect on the spiritual awakening process and releasing old pains.

But it takes courage.

It does. But if you dare to keep directing your attention to your vertical core, it's easier to be receptive, and being receptive makes it easier to let go of control. Letting go of control makes it easier to let go of your mistaken identification that you are a separate self who could be harmed.

I want to let go of control and surrender to the Divine flow of life and not be so protective of my image, but there are places within me where fear, limited thinking, and unworthiness still reside and stop me.

Let's unpack that.

Contemplative Question:
What is my experience when I rest my awareness in the center of my head?

Access this chapter's guided practice in the *Unshakable Inner Peace* course at: UnshakableSeries.com

CHAPTER SEVEN: LOSING CONTROL

Fear naturally arises when you try to give up control. Fear stems from the psychological process of the ego and the nervous system. The psyche is there to protect the image, the body, relationships, belongings, and the success you've already accrued. It doesn't want to let go until it knows something is there to help guide the way to something even better.

My ego hedges its bets when it comes to the unknown. It tries to figure out if surrendering is worth it. My mind constantly tries to determine if I'll be secure if I let the Divine take the lead. It seems to get worse as I age.

You feel you have more to lose now, and your psychological conditioning has had more years to take hold.

When I gave up my college degree at nineteen, I wasn't afraid of having no secure employment. When I pierced my nose and decided to become a professional singer, with no experience proving I could do that, I didn't doubt my future. Mum was the one that freaked out. But now, I'm caught directly between trying to control how my life will unfold and letting the Divine mystery take charge.

Once you recognize the light of your essential self, trying to give up control is unnecessary. Your essence can't control or be controlled. You will know this. This book will guide you and others toward the Light in themselves and away from this protective impulse that you allowed to run your life.

What do you mean by 'the Light?'

Love, non-judgment, peace, harmony, equanimity, surrender, knowing, non-resistance. The essence of the real you is Light. Your essence is already all these things. Our conversations can help you see that.

Great books on these subjects have already been written.

Well, good on you for giving up so soon. We're only a few writing sessions in.

You do sarcasm well.

I'll use anything to get your attention to where it needs to be. Do you see how the mind makes you give up so early when stepping into something new?

Yep. I see it in my friends and clients too. By the way, what is your name?

You can call me the Guiding Light.

That's not your name.

> It describes the energy of the voice you hear. I'm guiding you back to your fundamental essence, liberating you from the suffering your mind creates. You're about to lose control of who you think you are.

A thunderous wave crashed onto the rocks a mere fifty feet outside the room, triggering a wave of fear within me.

Losing control scares me. To say I'm going to give my life over to the Divine frightens me, even though that doesn't make logical sense because I trust in God and the interconnectivity of the Universe.

> Exactly what are you afraid of?

I'm scared I won't be able to create what I want and live how I want. I'm afraid that I'll be broke and become a bag lady after all the stories I've heard about enlightened masters being homeless at some point. I don't want that. I like throw pillows, hot stone massages, and matcha lattes too much. If I let go of control, I won't be able to steer my ship. I won't be able to say, "I want this or that." The Divine might take me down a road that makes me give up my entire personality. I will become dull and devoid of all personality. I will become a miniature version of who I am now. I'll become dull and lifeless after all the time I have put into developing my image, persona, public speaking, and presence. My presence will diminish. I'll become quiet and more monk-like. That's not how I see myself.

I pause to re-read my rant and realize I was unaware of these unconscious beliefs.

Do you think Jesus was dull?

No.

Do you think any of your spiritual teachers are boring?

Definitely not.

Then why are you worried about these things? Did they not have the heavens open and shower down on them the grandest impact, love, service, recognition, and support that you could ever imagine?

They did, but that is them, and I am just me.

You are grander in your capacity than you can even fathom. You are a bursting supernova of potential, creativity, and service you can't comprehend. Fear of letting go is normal. Letting go of the idea that you are a specific someone is one of the final frontiers of the spiritual journey. You can't stabilize your body, mind, and energy system to perceive the Infinite dimension without giving up the notion that you are this person that you currently identify with.

The untamed mind is a rival to realizing that your essential nature is not your personality, history, or name. It keeps you from being receptive. The human mind is a psychological process, and along with the body, it creates the belief that you are a separate self that needs to be defended. In the awakening process, you first learn to develop the observer who can watch the mind and not be identified with the mind's contents. If you can witness its contents and not get dragged into its drama, you can more easily drop into the internal space of your body. Your body is where emotions are felt. It's storage space for all the things that have happened to you that you had to cope with. The body and mind work together to avoid those bad things happening again. It creates all kinds of defenses to protect you.

What kind of defenses?

Not dropping your guard in relationships to prevent others from truly reaching your heart. Not speaking up for yourself because you don't want to rock the boat. Living in the mental realm most of the time or using food or substances to suppress your feelings. Creating an image you project out to the world when you feel different internally.

I notice individuals frequently choosing a defensive strategy that works best for them to keep them protected from discomfort, rejection, or harm.

These defenses keep the sense of a separate self that needs protection intact. Which one do you use most?

The one I'm more aware of lately is a contraction of the mind. When someone successful in business says I should do something I'm not doing, I often reject it. If I'm honest with myself, I don't dismiss it because it wouldn't work, or I feel they are steering me in the wrong direction for my lifestyle. I push against it because it would bring up my insecurities if I had to do what they were saying.

Good catch.

I can see how I've fooled myself by thinking I was right and somehow 'above' their prescription. In reality, I was too scared to spend more time on social media, fearing not putting forward the perfect image. I was too afraid to reach out to my network for support, fearing looking desperate. I even went so far as to judge them. I would say things to myself like, "That might work for them because they are not as authentic as me."

> You must descend into the body to fully experience your unlimited power. It's uncomfortable initially because past and present-day feelings reside there. But once you dare to feel rather than resist what shows up in the moment, the challenge of remaining in the body disappears.

If I had the humility to follow through with some of their business advice earlier, I would have had to sit with the insecure parts of me.

> That kind of courage assists you in knowing where you cut off the flow of abundant love and support that is there for you. You must go toward the fire of discomfort if you want to live in peaceful waters.

That reminds me of Rumi. He says

God's presence is there in front of me, a fire on the left, a lovely stream on the right.
One group walks toward the fire, into the fire, another toward the sweet flowing water.
No one knows which are blessed and which not.
Whoever walks into the fire appears suddenly in the stream.
A head goes under on the water's surface, that head pokes out of the fire. Most people guard against going into the fire, and so end up in it.
Those who love the water of pleasure and make it their devotion are cheated with this reversal.

My sense is the body is where one can release emotions, as well as impediments to love, and old traumas. But most guard against doing this kind of internal work, though I personally believe it is well worth it.

It can be challenging.

This psychological and somatic work has radically changed my life.

Once you master the ability to be still in the body and not suppress your experience or contract your life force in contact with anything or anyone—which essentially comes from being more receptive—you are ready for the next phase. Getting this far is a massive accomplishment and cause for celebration, but you're not done yet. The most significant surrender is yet to come.

What surrender is that?

> Letting go of the idea that you are a separate person by
> the name of Rachael Jayne. You are not the person you
> have thought or felt you were. You will realize there is no
> separateness between your essential nature and everyone
> else's.

Do you mean we are all one?

> Let's move into a greater understanding of this phrase.
> Otherwise, it can sound like new-age dogma. People
> resist the idea that they are not a person with a body, a
> personality, a soul, and thousands of thoughts daily,
> because those things make it feel like they are a separate
> person. You are aware of thoughts that arise in your mind
> rather than Datta's or your sister's. A unique psychological,
> physical, and soulful process happens through individual
> Earth Suits. It doesn't mean that the fundamental essence
> of the three of you is different. We are all one essential
> awareness looking through different prisms, called souls or
> people. Rachael Jayne, why do you resist the idea "we are
> all one?"

I have resistance because it often sounds like an intellectual concept
that's being parroted back from a book that a person has read and
is trying to sound more elevated than they are. When some people
say this, it doesn't feel connected to a deep knowing or embodied
experience that they are one with all. Maybe they are, and that's only

my judgment. Even though I believe we are all interconnected with one Infinite Divine Presence, I don't want to be a new-age parrot. I also believe that we are separate. I have an individual soul different from the person sitting next to me. I have an independent body and energy field that I must protect. So it's not that I am no one. I believe that we are all one in one sense, but we are all separate too. How do you explain that?

> It's true. We *are* all separate as well. Each bird is distinct from each rabbit, bobcat, tree, and human family member. But a unified field of consciousness and life force emanates through all, including the rock face that runs through your property, the pine trees in your front yard, and the river rock tiles around your bathtub. In one dimension, you'll feel separate, which is sometimes healthy, and in another, you will experience no breaks in the Infinite Divine Matrix. Peace comes when realizing how oneness is shared and how separateness is experienced. Life arises through multiple dimensions of experience. Don't resist any dimension. I'm not asking you to fight against the experience of a separate self. Just don't get stuck thinking that is who you are. You don't lose your soul when you surrender to the unified field of consciousness. You don't lose your personality. You don't lose your sense of humor. Do any spiritual teachers you follow look like they have lost their sense of humor?

No. Even Eckart Tolle, who many find not that exciting of a presenter, can be hilarious.

That's what I'm talking about. Have you noticed that you have gotten funnier the more you have let go into your spiritual journey?

Well, I feel more uninhibited and less self-conscious now. Funny comments spring forth easier these days.

When the ego stops protecting, you move into the 'flow state' and become funnier. The more you let go of control, the more animated you become. To do this, you must become more receptive. Receptivity is the opposite of control. Imagine that your fist is tight. That's control. Now think of your hand relaxed and open to receive. That's letting go of control. You must train the mind and body to let go in order to move through the portal toward lasting inner peace.

I need to train my mind and body, because I can still feel them freaking out about letting go and simply receiving. My thoughts tell me I will become dull and personality-less, like all those images of enlightened masters sitting silently in front of a room and not saying much. They don't look like they are living an exciting life.

They listen with no agenda from the front of the room. You do the same in your work all the time. You listen with no agenda to those who come to the microphone at your retreats. You often stand instead of sitting in a guru chair most of the time. Your insight is quick because you know people and ego patterns and can talk about them eloquently. You may have an outdated view of what an enlightened person looks like.

So what *does* a modern enlightened person look like? The answer to that might help me relax.

....

Contemplative Question:
In what dimension am I separate, and in what dimension am I Infinite?

Access this chapter's guided practice in the *Unshakable Inner Peace* course at: UnshakableSeries.com

CHAPTER EIGHT:
EGO TRAPS

Do enlightened masters need a lot of time in stillness?

> No, because they are already in a place of inner stillness. Time alone in silence is, by all means, helpful to continue their spiritual practices. However, stillness and silence are more important for people on their way to the embodied understanding that their essential self is still and silent.

Does an enlightened master need a lot of time to train their mind?

> They've already trained themselves to not believe they are their mind. They have stabilized their focus on their essential self, so they don't need training for enlightenment. However, they can train their mind for other skills. They might want to learn speed reading, improve their memory, manifest through visualization focus, or be more strategic for a project they care about. How you formulate this question about training the mind shows me you're missing an essential understanding of how the process of awakening works.

Can you tell me more about that?

The word "training" can easily lead a spiritual student on a wild goose chase. You need to train yourself not to believe that you are your thoughts. You don't need to train your mind to stay quiet. Living from the Infinite dimension where peace permanently resides is about training attention and focus versus training the mind to be silent or think positive thoughts. The mind is less trainable than most give it credit for. Think of an old dog that's never been trained in any way. It can be near impossible to teach it any new tricks. Hence, many spiritual seekers are stuck, year after year, decade after decade, in the same old mind traps. The mind is a highly conditioned psychological process. Your mind, my dear, has a mind of its own.

Do enlightened masters still need time to practice sitting without any resistance? For example, not trying to get rid of discomfort, pain, or negative emotion.

A lot of the time? No. Some of the time? Yes. They experience enlightenment because they can feel their unshakable still essence in the face of any pain. Through periods of grief, trauma, or unexpected change, they might need time to process what happened. They still have Earth suits to be kind to.

I believe enlightened masters are very humble. Does a person need a lot of time to train themselves to let go of their need to be unique, significant, or needed by others?

Those words represent what the ego wants to be. It's challenging to train the ego to let go of these needs. Instead, train your focus to move from the ego mind to the essential nature of your Being. After training your focus enough, attention will eventually remain without conscious effort in what we've been calling that third dimension of awareness. Once that occurs, believing the ego mind is impossible, and suffering evaporates. Enlightenment is not about being free from the ego. The ego is a physical-psychological process that gives you a sense that you are separate from others, which is a healthy part of human life. When someone lives in this higher stage of consciousness, they act with no resistance to others or to what happens in the world, so there is little need to feel unique, significant, or needed by others. The level of non-resistance a spiritual master lives with, and these ego needs, have a hard time existing simultaneously.

Thanks for clarifying. I intuit that I'm not crossing into the next dimension of consciousness because I don't comprehend what is specifically needed for this next phase. Conversations on enlightenment can be full of spiritual jargon as we speak beyond our experience.

You're right. The mind analyzes. As the genuine impulse for spiritual awakening grows more robust, the ego-mind will try to hijack the spiritual impulse to let go and be present. It will analyze and control. It will try to make you think that the ego is what is becoming more enlightened. The ego can become more functional, healthy, and less triggered by others, but will never become enlightened. The mind tries to maintain its position that it is a person who will become enlightened and get a gold star at the end of it.

I can feel my ego doing that when you put it that way. It wants recognition.

> Enlightenment is not for the few. It can be for the masses. We can see this in a shorter period if people are shown the map. You have only been shown *part* of the map. Most people are not shown the whole map, making it difficult to shift into this truly peaceful dimension, especially when the ego tries to hijack the process.

Some have been shown the map through a religious or spiritual tradition. It is easier to see the exact map if the directions come without dogmatic or mythological stories. In my Catholic upbringing, I received outdated translations of what was meant by the prophets who spoke messages centuries ago. I'm learning from you that we can only understand the spiritual process through the set of eyes and ears we currently use. The key is which eyes I see with. I need to keep asking myself, "Am I seeing this with my ego's eyes or my higher-dimensional eyes?"

> It's hard to hear spiritual teachings in the way they were intended because, usually, they come through lower-dimension minds translating higher-dimension concepts. You get stuck because you don't have a mentor to

describe what is required and light the path when you fall for an ego trap. You don't know how to stay receptive when it gets tricky. You fixate on the spiritual practices that are already easy for you and avoid ones you don't understand.

I'm not exactly sure how I do that, though I take your word for it. It's easier to see it in others. Some defend themselves by shutting out the world, detaching from people, meditating, or living a monastic life. They mistake that for progress because they have heard that being 'unattached' is a supreme state of Being. I think that can be a trap. The defense pattern of the one who feels like the monk life is the way to enlightenment can be to withdraw from the aliveness or messiness of the present moment, move up into their head and away from others. This happens due to the deep-seated and often unconscious fear of being overwhelmed or intruded upon by others.

Those who like to keep things harmonious all the time can quickly do something to calm their body down, manage their impulses, and push their life force down, so they don't feel upset. Their defense pattern is to keep the peace and guard against feeling anger at any cost.

Yes. At that moment, their ego's need for feeling peaceful keeps them stuck in the dimension of the separate self versus knowing their essence is peace, even in chaos. It might appear on the surface that they are going to a peaceful place, but often they are not. They are calming their Earth suit down by numbing out somehow or suppressing their natural reaction.

I have more examples of how the ego hijacks the awakening process.

Let's hear them.

Those who always want to feel happy and positive try to move away from pain by mentally re-framing things that cause them to hurt or be frustrated. When a mental re-frame is used to escape pain, for example, "I don't think they were suitable for me anyhow," which might be used after a breakup, it doesn't allow authentic, full emotions to be present. The re-frame is essentially a defense mechanism. It's hard to catch this because it can be so subtle. A person who re-frames quickly can resist their present moment experience by putting their attention in the mental realm to escape.

Keep going. You're on a roll.

On the other hand, those who place great importance on feeling emotions can get caught up in their emotional experience and believe they *are* their emotions. When I've questioned people during a coaching session, I've heard, "But I feel this" or "I feel that," indicating that it *has* to be true. They think emotion is a higher form of message than thoughts. It can be, but often emotion is the Earth suit's habitual reaction based on experience. It's a trap to think I can listen to my emotions more than my thoughts because they are somehow more spiritual. Both are highly conditioned experiences.

Some people don't feel their emotions, some suppress them, some spiritually bypass them, some ignore them, and some dramatize those emotions and blow them up to be bigger than they need to be, so it becomes more about the story than being present with the feeling.

Humans go toward what feels safe for them, like moths to the proverbial flame. A person can easily think they are doing something to progress spiritually. However, that behavior keeps them in their ego's preference, which may come in the form of being alone, being in harmony, being with pleasure, being in their mental realm, or listening to their feelings over everything. You must be able to go toward what feels scary as well. Awakening to the next stage of consciousness is like death. The idea that the essence of you is a separate self dies. You've heard that before, haven't you?

I have. From what you said earlier, I understand that the awakening process is about losing the sense that I am someone and instead realizing that I am not the person I thought. Because it hasn't happened yet, I don't quite understand it, and it feels unsettling.

I understand why it is scary. Turning towards the potential of becoming a nobody isn't attractive to the mind when its job has been to build you into somebody since you were born. But the death of the separate self's identity is not a fearful process for your essential self. Do you see how your mind continually tries to hijack your awakening experience?

I see multiple ways that I do this.

Please pause right there. When you say, "I see multiple ways I do this," that is an incorrect analysis. You don't do it. The mind, which creates the sense of a separate self, does it.

Thanks. I appreciate the clarification.

It's essential to continue seeing your mind as not who you are.

Thank you for the reminder. I see how my mind hijacks the spiritual awakening process by always thinking about the future. I'm constantly working with tools to improve myself, so I can be more of who I want to be in the future.

That's not necessarily a bad thing. You can work to become a better human for the future, so why is this a limitation in spiritual awakening?

I want to improve myself, but personal development is limited if I want to realize myself as something other than a separate self.

Very good.

I've been focused on practices that have helped me form a strong sense of a separate self with good boundaries, individual solid desires, and work ethic but don't necessarily help me wake up from the illusion that I am a separate self.

You're right. There's nothing wrong with these tools that tap you into your superpowers and become a dialed-in manifestor. Still, if the practices only help your ego get healthier, and don't lead you to realize that the ego is not who you are, then you will not experience the constant peace and organic joy you want.

I've been consumed with how to manifest my dreams. Not just small goals but extraordinary ones. I see that my need to create great things has made my seeking mind lead the show. I always seek the next grand experience. What feels like death is to stop seeking and be okay with the ordinary. I need to be joyful while washing dishes, checking email, and finding pleasure in daily tasks. I also admit that I'm an image-focused person. It feels like death to allow myself to be a person who isn't stylish or unique in some way. It's embarrassing, but I would prefer to fast for a week rather than be forced to wear a white T-shirt and no-label blue jeans in a room where I must interact with people. I could only do it if the white T-shirt had some bling around the neck and I could pair the jeans with hot pink pumps.

> To be seen by others in a desired way is an ego pattern that will loosen its grip when you realize that you are safe no matter what anyone thinks of you.

I love that. I understand we have human needs to survive and be happy. We need security, mystery, significance, love, and connection. Do these pose a problem in the awakening process?

> These needs should not be judged as bad or problematic, but are things to be aware of. It's helpful to become aware of these needs to get them filled in healthy ways. However, enlightenment is knowing you are already the essence of safety, mystery, significance, love, and connection. You don't need to attain what you already are.

Are you saying that to get to a place of enlightenment, you must give up all need to be significant?

Yes.

Do I have to give up all need to be loved?

Yes.

Do I have to give up all need to be secure?

Yes.

Do I have to give up all need to be both certain and uncertain?

Yes. Those weren't the answers you were hoping for, were they?

No, they weren't. I'm not sure why I'm shocked. I've heard similar things said by enlightened masters before.

You must understand that living in an enlightened state is a paradox. You have realized you are nobody and everybody and an individual at the same time. This relates to these needs also. The more you practice feeling secure, the more you know you don't need security. It's who you are. The more you practice receiving love, the more you realize you don't need love. It's who you are. Human needs are not to be thrown out the window, yet the ego can get stuck constantly seeking and grasping for these things. Whatever you do, remember the ego is not bad, so it's not about getting rid of your ego. The Infinite Self needs the ego to experience itself through a human form. If we didn't have an ego, we would not be able to wake up within these bodies and create in this ever-expanding Universe.

I like the way you said that. I've seen the ego get a bad rap in many spiritual circles.

We need a structure for the Divine to flow through and manifest. Therefore, you created a physical body and a psychological system to support that.

I like calling it my 'Earth Suit.'

It's a good call. It's not you, but is integral to your survival, just like a space suit is needed in space. It's a beautiful tool, but remember this warning: as you awaken, the separate self will try to hijack the process as it thinks it's the one that's evolving and deserves a gold star for how good it is on the spiritual path.

How will I know if it's doing that?

You'll see . . . if you are open to seeing.

Contemplative Question:
Have I carefully considered whether any of the following statements true?

- It is more spiritual not to express anger than to get angry at someone.
- Re-framing negative thoughts into positive ones is more spiritual than remaining negative.
- Feeling emotions is more spiritual than ignoring them.
- Detaching from others is more spiritual than feeling intimately connected to the messiness of relationships.

Access this chapter's guided practice in the *Unshakable Inner Peace* course at: UnshakableSeries.com

CHAPTER NINE: UNWORTHINESS

People call the unobserved mind the 'monkey mind' for good reason as it jumps from tree to tree, never still. This creates all sorts of fears, sensations, and emotions as the psychological structure of the mind tries to keep us safe, secure, loved, and approved of. When you teach, you use a great analogy and practice that helps people pay less attention to their monkey minds.

Which analogy do you mean?

Imagine you're in the ocean on a sunny day. Your head is above water, and your mind chatter moves above the water as well. You can hear the chatter clearly like a friend constantly talking to you when you only want to enjoy the water. When you ask your friend to be quiet, that doesn't work. If you tried to drown your friend, they would kick and scream, making you feel terrible. When you stopped pushing them down, they would rush to the water's surface again to catch their breath.

So, you're saying to not battle with the mind? I think I get it. Duck your head under the surface and enjoy the water. The mind's chatter will be above the water and sound like "burble, burble, burble." If you allow the voice to be above the water, it sounds cute, like some character from The Muppets.

That is a wonderful analogy, which I am sure will help me often. Peace never comes when I resist my mind. When I start judging that I can't control my mind, it only makes things louder. I love the idea of allowing the mental chatter to be above the water and relaxing under the water.

> At the risk of repeating myself, I want to say again that the end of suffering—caused by the mind—doesn't end when you resist the mind but when you shift focus to a different dimension of awareness. You've heard that where your attention goes, energy flows. Attention is something you can train. You can go to the gym to build muscle and get fitter. You can also build mental, physical, energetic, and emotional muscles that stabilize your core so you can always be aware of the third dimension.

Can you give me an example of building a strong mental muscle?

> When you have the thought, "I'm not worthy of writing this book," which I have noticed five times in the last five minutes is a great example.

Five times? I thought it was a constant drone.

When you focus on not being worthy of writing this book, you're building a mental muscle of unworthiness. You strengthen your unworthiness, making it easier to think that thought again. Is that what you want?

Definitely not. Especially when you put it that way, I don't want the thought that I am unworthy to come so easy.

Just to confirm, the more you focus on thoughts of your unworthiness—which are simply thoughts that arise without your consent—the easier those thoughts will take over your attention in the future. Instead, let the thought appear and disappear on the screen of awareness on its own. Don't try to think specific thoughts, as that is impossible. Just don't focus on that thought with your attention. Let it float on by. If you focus on the thought "I am not worthy," it will become your felt experience and drive behaviors that will support that belief.

When you put it that way, I never want to think that thought again. But I think that's easier said than done.

There is no problem if you think that thought again. The key is what you do with your focus when it arises without your expressed permission. Let it fly by like a butterfly. You can't train the mind never to have a particular thought again, but you can train the self-aware observer to not focus on the thought and judge it as problematic.

Great point. I need to train my focus instead of my thoughts. All these years, I've misunderstood the process. I thought seeing and noticing the thought and working out where it came from was essential. I estimate that 70% of my clients stop themselves from pursuing their dreams because they have to pinpoint why negative thoughts keep arising. I hear someone say, "I first need to find out the root cause of this fear and clear it out" often. That has never felt right to me.

> Thoughts that arise from past conditioning are not the issue. The problem is only when you get stuck in the mud with them. The practice is watching thoughts float by without touching or becoming entangled with them. If you don't stir them up by over-processing them, your nervous system won't respond to the old pattern as much. Eventually, that knee-jerk response will lose all power and not be agitated again by that thought passing by.

That sounds like freedom to me! When I ask myself what I could achieve if I didn't have the underlying "I am not worthy" internal message, a feeling of awe lifts me.

> You could achieve a great deal. Perhaps more than you can imagine. The most outstanding achievement would be the constant peace of mind when you know you're worthy and don't have to prove it.

Wow. That would be lovely. That thought relaxes me.

> You *are* worthy. Do you realize that?

Sometimes. But then I get caught in doubt. Many of my clients struggle with this too. They don't feel worthy, so they put the brakes on and don't move forward with what they want. Their hearts are in the right place, but they can't connect to their brilliance long enough to create momentum with action. They feel their potential in one moment and their lack of power in another.

> It's not easy for a human being to stay focused on their worthiness, but it's in reach when you train your focus away from the monkey mind and onto the spiritual dimension. Most people are not in environments that show us how or that put this quest high enough on the list of growth priorities.

What would it be like to have everyone's top priority be to embody unshakable inner peace? What would change if our schools, workplaces, and homes became vehicles to make this happen? Wouldn't that be cool?

> Yes, and it will be like that in the future. You'll live in a society with an education like this. We don't have enough masters to lobby for and teach this currently. That will change. You are doing this with The Awakened School. You prioritize living an awakened life and helping others do the same. It starts with intention. When the intention is there, the path is shown. When the student is ready, the teacher arrives. You declared five months ago enlightenment was the goal. You had the guts to tell your husband, and mentors have already shown up, and here we are discussing this in depth.

Telling Datta was hard. I just wanted him to be happy for me and inspired. Maybe he is, but he didn't show it. I wanted to talk to him more about my journey but was afraid of his skepticism.

> You and your journey inspire Datta, but sometimes he feels his job is to challenge you. Understand that your spiritual experience differs from his. Everyone experiences spirituality in their way. Sometimes, people believe their way is *the* way. There'll always be those who have a different upbringing than you, have read various spiritual texts, and have been steeped in other spiritual communities than you. They may think you are slightly off track because it doesn't fit their view of spirituality. I'm not saying this is the case with Datta, but you should prepare yourself for this.

How do I know if I'm on or off track?

> You're on the right track if you experience more peace without repressing or avoiding anything. You're on the right track if you become less judgmental. You're on the right track if you experience yourself less as a personality and more connected to the Infinite matrix of life. You're off track if you feel it's your job to save others from their ego. Let people have their beliefs about enlightenment and how to get there, while you focus on your own experience. If you feel less receptive to any moment, you are off track. Very soon, it will become clear that something has shifted from this conversation

because you will experience the difference. They'll also be people who think you're a little arrogant with this goal, so be mindful of who you tell.

How can you tell me to be mindful of who I tell? I'm writing this book about my desire for enlightenment. The cat will soon be well and truly out of the freaking bag!

Yes, but the people who have picked up this book and have read this far are on your side. They too, have made a courageous decision to put their spiritual awakening higher on their priority list. Their sincere intention is to end the suffering caused by their mind. Most of the readers of this book don't tell many others about their intentions either. You've told your husband and one close friend but no one else. I don't recommend telling anyone that cannot hold you in the highest light and support you. Keep it to yourself, keep it contained, and keep yourself humble.

What is humility, really?

When humility or any spiritual virtue is experienced, you feel expansive and light. You, my dear, make the mistake of trying to be humble so people won't judge you as arrogant. Don't try to be humble. Instead, feel the energy of humility.

I don't know if it's easy to feel what the energy of humility feels like, rather than trying to force humility. I don't want people to think I'm up myself.

What is humility to you, Rachael Jayne?

I think it's realizing that I am no better or more special than anyone else. I may have fewer layers of protection around me, but that doesn't mean I'm any better. In humility, I don't need others to think that I am unique, but I don't shy away from my authority and wisdom when the moment calls for it. Have to call attention to all the wonderful things I think I do. It feels quiet and knowing, and no one needs to see what I experience on the inside.

> Exactly. You don't need Datta or anyone else to understand your experience. When you feel a strong need for someone to understand what you're going through, you are experiencing your protective ego-self.

I often come from ego, so what qualifies me to write this book?

> There is that unworthiness again.

I can't help it if I don't think I'm up for this job.

> But you *can* help it. What are you trying to deny? That you are not receptive enough? Need to be more spiritual? Need to be more open and evolved?

No, I can claim all those things. It feels more like I am not worthy enough.

> Unworthiness is an illusion and figment of the separate self. Just watch it float on by through your awareness. Don't talk about it. Please don't touch it. Let it play in the next room.

I guess that means to stop trying to get rid of the thought I am not worthy? If I wanted to eliminate it, that would be touching it.

> Exactly. As I've said before, where your attention goes, energy flows. When training the mental muscle of focus, first become aware of the thought. Then move to the second dimension of awareness, the observer of the thought. That gives you some space not to touch the thought but to watch it. It's hard not to fixate on the original thought because, for decades, you've trained your focus to be on the monkey mind. It's hard to break. Hence, working out with the muscle of focus is a must. Once you see the two dimensions, the thought and the observer, you have a clear choice of where you want to focus in that mental gym session. It will start to get as simple as, do I focus on my right hand or left hand? Do I focus on the thought or the observer?
> Once you have become expert at changing focus from thought to the observer, you can shift your focus to the third dimension, which is the awareness that is aware of the observer.

I want to eliminate these thoughts of unworthiness because I want to create my dream life. Manifesting cool things gives me a taste of feeling worthy, but I know it doesn't lead to constantly feeling worthy.

You can go directly to the inherent worthiness and peace you are, without creating anything different in your life. It's about focusing on the spiritual rather than perfecting the human dimension. As you focus on stillness and presence, you are there.

I assume that's what people mean when they say "You don't have to do anything. You're already enlightened." Nothing needs to manifest for us to experience our true nature. It's already there. It's our shadow side that hides it from us.

That is partly true. You don't have to do or have anything to feel a state of equilibrium whenever you want. You can go to that now. But it's not as simple as saying everyone is already enlightened. There are things you need to be open to for inner peace to remain consistent in your experience. The mind will still play its tricks to keep you from taking a deep breath and knowing that life carries you and holds you. It keeps you tightly wound to thoughts like "I need to do certain things before I can take a deep breath and relax."

I can relate. I've fallen into that trap my entire life. The desire to not feel unworthy has driven my choices, behaviors, and ambitions, leading to too much effort and working way too hard.

It's good you own up to that. But remember, your salvation doesn't come when you become perfect enough to be given an 'I am worthy' trophy. It comes when you have trained your focus to remain on your essential nature, which has always been worthy.

You may be getting through to me. It's about where I put my focus.

Yes. That will enable you to take the deep breaths you need to relax into your higher self. Relaxation of your body opens the doorway to receptivity. It's easier to experience the dimension of Infinite Presence when you don't hold your breath or tighten up. The less you constrict, the more you receive. The more receptive you are, the easier it is to focus on your essential nature. Adults rarely take even one deep breath per day. You must be open-minded in your body, not just your mind.

But when I relax my belly, emotions that I've repressed can surface, which is anything but relaxing.

Emotions that arise are a release of resistance. Don't judge emotions as good or bad. Like thoughts, you allow them to be and move through. Let them be known and be felt but don't do anything with them. Don't peer deeply within them and process them.

Isn't turning our attention toward feelings and away from the monkey mind important?

It's a little complicated. Let's talk about that.

Contemplative Question:
Where has my focus been today?

- Has it been on my thoughts and feelings?
- Has it been on the observer who comments on thoughts and feelings?
- Has it been on the awareness that is aware of the observer yet doesn't comment?

Access this chapter's guided practice in the *Unshakable Inner Peace* course at: UnshakableSeries.com

CHAPTER TEN:
INTENSE EMOTIONS

What is the best way to process emotions?

What do you mean by 'process? Would you say that means figuring out where the emotion came from, looking at the belief tied to the feeling, and seeing it in a new light so that the emotional reaction won't happen again?

That sounds about right.

Then it would be good to use the word "allow" instead of "process." When you allow an emotion to be, it can move through your Earth suit quicker, causing less suffering. You don't need to engage your head to figure out where that emotion came from. Don't look toward emotion to analyze it. Think of emotion as energy in motion. If you stop to think about an emotion, tell a story about it, or believe you have to feel the depths of it to understand the root cause of why it's arising, that is actually a form of resistance.

I've done that a lot. I call it 'The curse of over-processing.' I have thought that feeling my feelings deeply to figure out why they were arising in the first place was what was needed to awaken.

On the one hand, it is. Don't suppress your feelings, but don't grasp them, either. Don't try to bring an emotion closer to your mental awareness than needed. If emotion is felt with presence and breath, it can move and won't get sticky.

The more receptive your body, the more these emotions will move through you as they open and clear your energy field. Being receptive supports your system to unwind emotional habits that tend to happen in a knee-jerk fashion. If you are closed to emotions, your energy field will get heavier.

Allowing an emotion means to:

- Allow yourself to notice the emotion that arises.
- Experience the sensations of the emotion without suppressing anything.
- With the help of your self-aware observer, notice you have some distance between the emotion and the observer.
- Stabilize your focus toward the self-aware observer and unconditional presence while allowing any residue of the emotion to move through you.

It doesn't mean to stir the emotions by feeling them so deeply that you think the emotion is you, the way you think you are your thoughts sometimes. Emotions are habits for the most part. Situation A happens, and we feel happy. Situation B happens, and we feel sad. Emotions are highly conditioned responses until they are not. When you see the ingrained habits, you can catch them earlier, not dive into them or 'process them.'

I may need clarification about when to feel emotions and when not to.

> Let's start with when to not focus on the emotional realm too much because it can keep old emotional habits in place.
>
> • Don't focus on emotions that stem from unwanted mental habits. If you do, you will keep the emotional habit in place as well as the mental habit. For example, if you are used to critical thoughts about others, you'll continue to feel frustrated and angry. Don't focus on feeling that frustration and anger.
>
> • Don't focus on emotions that stem from your conditioned nervous system. If you do, you will keep the emotional habit and the nervous system's reaction to the environment firmly in place.
>
> For example, if you're used to feeling anxious in the body, you'll continue to feel anxious. Don't focus on that anxiety by psychoanalyzing it.

I know my emotional habits are disappointment and sadness. They come from thoughts of lack and dissatisfaction. Are you saying that if I allowed the emotion of sadness to take over, that would keep the habit of sadness in place?

> It would all depend on if you truly allowed the movement of sadness without processing, resisting, or judging, or if you felt it but tried to stir it up by analyzing it.

Can I use an example that happened to me to see if we can further unpack this?

Of course. Examples are always good. It makes understanding easy.

Once, I accidentally picked up dumbbells that were too heavy for me. They were in kilos and not pounds, given I was visiting Australia, and as a result I hurt my back.

Let me stop you right there. There is no such thing as an accident.

How would you not call that an accident, given that it hurt my back quite badly?

Was it possibly an important lesson not to push?

Maybe. That week I had yet to come to terms with where I needed boundaries and where I needed to rest. I knew the weight was too heavy for me after my first squat. My back didn't give way until the fourth squat.

When I realized that my back was injured, tears began to form even before I could tell myself the 'woe is me' story I had on repeat from the past when I had to live with a disabling back injury. I could see the emotional process happening in real-time. I didn't go into my habit of processing my emotions or giving them attention. I didn't let the tears fully form and drizzle down my cheeks.

Yes, but you allowed this emotional movement of energy.

Really? It felt more like I chose not to give it attention.

You didn't push it away or suppress it or bring it closer to you than needed. You didn't ask yourself, "Why does this always keep happening?"

Just like a thought, it came in and went out. If you do not contract against the emotion, they will move by or 'release' as people like to say. It isn't very helpful when you or other spiritual seekers use the word release. It insinuates that there is something to get rid of, and as soon as the mind concludes there is something to release, you are in resistance. Therefore, allowing is more accurate. Allowing is what fosters the unwinding of old patterns that are caused by constricted energy.

That's big! I need to remember that.

Yes, you do. To allow means to have a direct experience of the present moment.

What about intense emotion that wants to be felt deeply and then released? The type of emotion that feels like it's coming out of left field? It's like an unconscious part of me is becoming conscious, bringing with it a lot of emotion.

That's right. Something arises to become conscious.

Do I allow myself to have those emotions fully?

To allow means to be in the present moment, in the mystery, and to give up mental control of what should and shouldn't occur, so it's a difficult question to answer in a way that most people will understand, but here it goes.

- Allow yourself to notice the emotion that arises. Allow the feeling to arise in your awareness and body.

- Experience the sensations of that emotion without suppressing anything. Allow the sensations to be present throughout your body, but don't do anything to suppress or calm them down. When you try to calm them down with your breath, you're not allowing the emotion to move through. This emotion is trying to find its way up and out of your unconscious. It's been resisted for quite a while. In the past, your heart contracted against an emotion that wanted to surface, and now it's coming out. Let it run its course. If it wants to be felt fully, let it. If it wants to cry for a moment, let it. Allowing its expression will inform you whether you need to feel it more. Emotion is energy in emotion, and much of it has built up because it wasn't allowed to be expressed earlier in life, so it can be intense when it finally comes up.

- With the help of your self-aware observer, notice that you have some distance between the emotion and the observer. Notice that you have two places you can put your focus: either on the emotions or the observer that is present to the emotions.

- Stabilize your focus toward the self-aware observer and unconditional presence while allowing any residue of the emotion to move through you. Keep bringing your focus back to the unconditional presence of the observer as any final sensations have their way through your body.

I guess being on a spiritual path requires you to be excellent at standing in the fire of uncomfortable feelings.

That's because when you contract or resist against an emotion, you worsen it. When people stay stuck in an emotion, it creates a contraction against their life force. When a kink is present in a coiled garden hose, you move toward the hose to release the kink. With buried emotion, you move your awareness toward the feeling, not away from it. You don't have to search and dig for the stuck parts of you that are stuck. They will show up on your doorstep sooner or later. They will arise when you are ready to meet them. The impulse towards wholeness is so strong that this kink will unwind itself at some point. There is no need for 'over-processing' and searching.

Is allowing negative emotion the way we can deal with healing from trauma?

Healing from trauma requires a strong understanding of the body, brain, and human survival instinct and how it all works together. In trauma, something very primal went wrong. The person may have witnessed a tragic death, experienced an accident, was tortured, was held down and couldn't escape, or perhaps had been abused somehow and couldn't get away. Trauma can have many faces. However, the primal energies of fear, fight, flight, and freeze stunted in every one of those faces. The brain-body connection cannot be overlooked.

I think this is an important topic because millions of people—and animals for that matter—are trapped in a trauma response and do not feel safe allowing emotion. There is much to cover on this topic, but I think it's different than the one we are exploring on enlightenment.

> It's related and different. For more people to awaken, resolving trauma response must become an absolute priority for every culture. But I'm happy to return to our more present conversation about you and your awakening.

You make me sound like a Diva.

> Because you are.

Is it bad to be a Diva?

> Not at all. But you are a Diva, and you're not a Diva. You have mastered your ability to put yourself at the center of your life, look after yourself, and have a healthy sense of selfishness. You are also a generous, service-oriented person here to help many people feel stronger about themselves.

Thank you. I appreciate that.

So many appreciate you for the way you are. You are deeply loved by many who "get" you.

What about feeling positive emotions? I'm sure many others like me have been taught that it's not always safe to feel happier than someone else and may not allow themselves positive emotions. For example, what if someone lived with a family member who was depressed and had to lower their vibration to stay connected to that person. I've seen where resistance to joy happens too.

> Indeed, it does. Having a more receptive body makes you less resistant to positive emotions. Don't grasp either the positive or the negative emotions. Don't try to pull positive emotions closer to you. When the thought comes, "I have to stay in this happy and peaceful place all the time," joy will lessen.

So, I shouldn't try to be happier and lift myself into more positive emotions?

> I'm not saying that. To have the intention of being a more joyful person is a great thing, but as soon as you are upset when joy is elusive, you are in resistance. Don't try to aim for everything to always be peaceful and joyful. That's a trap. Can you feel the difference between when you don't want joy to leave your experience and when you freely allow whatever is moving through you to have its place?

It feels more conditional when I don't want joy to leave. I think I've somehow failed if I'm not feeling optimistic. I also feel constriction in my body when I cut off the flow of emotion. I sometimes cry when I'm thrilled or feel so much love, but if I resist it, my throat tenses, and my face contorts. My mind sends a signal to my brain, that feeling this emotion is unsafe. How can I get more comfortable with emotion and not shut it off? I cry easily and lose myself in feelings that look intense to others. My depth of emotion is embarrassing.

> Yet that depth of emotion is beautiful. Whenever you feel emotion, you inspire others to touch theirs. Inner peace is not about being devoid of feeling. You will experience a lovely equanimity much of the time, but there will be times when you feel more emotion than most. You feel more joy because you are more open, but the other side of that is— because you have more empathy and compassion—you'll feel sad when you see hurt.

That's why I can't watch the violent or suspenseful movies I used to watch. My system is too sensitive—unless it's Matt Damon where I can focus on his muscles.

> I won't tell Datta.

That's funny, but he already knows.

I just had an interesting experience with a friend's emotions this morning, and now I'm unsure if I did the right thing.

> Describe what happened.

Datta and I saw a post on Facebook where someone wrote negatively about a friend of ours. We alerted him, given he's in the public eye and hundreds would have seen it. He said he felt angry and betrayed because he had done much for this person. We could all feel the energy of vengeance in this woman's post. In this situation, should I try not to feel anger and remember my Infinite nature or should I feel my upset?

> Great question. Your feelings follow your thoughts. What was your primary idea about the situation?

I thought "This woman must feel much pain to lash out like this." I felt for her because acting like this would hurt *her* reputation, not our friend's. Because I had compassion for her, I didn't feel triggered, vengeful, or overly protective of my friend.

> If, instead, you thought, "What a bitch, she's wrong to do this," would you have had anger arise?

Yes, I think so.

> That's right. Your friend felt hurt because he thought "I did so much for her," but at that moment felt used and mistreated. But it's okay that he feels sad or angry. Remember, it's just energy moving through him. If you can feel it with no justification, drama, or vengeance, it will move through and won't create the habit of needing to feel those negative emotions in the future.

We've covered much ground today, and I'm delighted that we have this time together.

I'm here for you.

But who are you? I would love to know.

Get some good rest. We'll pick this up in the morning.

Keep me hanging, why don't you?

This wouldn't be as fun if I couldn't tease you a little along the way.

Do you have a name?

Yes.

What's your name? What do I call you?

You can call me whatever you like. I will call you "She who doesn't give up."

No, really, who are you? My higher self? An enlightened master that has passed on?

I don't want to tell you who I am yet.

Really?

Really. People worry too much about what higher dimension they are talking to or are receiving information from. You will be too much in your head if I tell you. I don't want that to cloud our conversation.

I see the wisdom in that.

Good. I'll explain more about who I am and my relationship with you as we go deeper into this conversation. I first want you to feel the uninterrupted flow of hearing my voice and writing what you hear.

Will you tell me who you are before we finish this book?

I promise.

Fine. I'll let you off the hook for now.

You were only hooking yourself. Get some good rest. Tomorrow will be a little more intense.

Seriously?

Seriously!

Well, on that note . . . goodnight.

Contemplative Question:
In what ways do I not "allow" my emotions?

Access this chapter's guided practice in the *Unshakable Inner Peace* course at: UnshakableSeries.com

CHAPTER ELEVEN:
UNWINDING RESISTANCE

I open a blank Word document, and the blinking cursor reminds me that writer's block can strike anytime. Maybe I won't be greeted by the voice today. In an attempt to stop my doubting mind, I type, "Writing isn't a hobby for me. It's a calling."

The call had gotten stronger over the years. I published my first book, *Powerful and Feminine*, in 2011. It took me nearly five years to complete, as I interrupted my writing flow with uncertainty about my writing style and whether my message was worthwhile to anyone. In contrast, the first draft of my second book, *Divine Breadcrumbs*, was written in 3 straight days as I was determined not to let thoughts of unworthiness interrupt me until that first draft was complete. At the end of those three days, I felt one of the most incredible highs of my life. Writing in a receptive mode for that long helped me go far beyond my rational and judgmental mind. *Divine Breadcrumbs* was not the book I thought I would write. It poured out unimpeded and surprised the heck out of me. It was a memoir of my life's most embarrassing, thrilling, and challenging times in my search for true love and spiritual awakening.

Now, in Hawaii, I must complete the first draft of my third book, *Unshakable Inner Peace*. I intended to be fully open to the mystery of what would find its way to the page, but as I woke up on day two of the writing retreat, I had doubts about surrendering my keyboard to the unknown. I stared at the hand-written pages at chronicled a conversation with a voice in my head about how I could reach enlightenment this lifetime. *Where was this book taking me? What were my readers going to think? What will my husband think?*

> Everything is going to be okay. Just pretend no one will ever read this. This time is simply for us to write together and enjoy the lessons for your personal and spiritual journey. If it ever gets into the hands of someone, they will receive value because they have similar questions and challenges. Your questions are more refined as time goes on. The deeper you go into the awakening process, the more nuanced your understanding must be. The spiritual awakening process is like living in one paradox after another.

The spiritual journey is full of contradictions.

> That's because when we speak about one dimension of awareness, something can be true, yet in another, it may be the opposite.

Okay. One contradiction I've wrestled with is desire. Do I need to give up all desire and not want anything to become enlightened? Or should I learn spiritual tools and techniques to manifest my version of heaven on earth?

We'll get to all of it. We'll talk about the paradox of desire. We'll discuss shadow work, embodiment, and how much meditation time is warranted. We'll talk more about focus, self-control, and how the awakening process is like becoming a world-class musician or athlete. Self-control must come first. I mean control of the ego-self; otherwise, you will never relax enough for the True Self to emerge.

So, am I channeling this book?

My question was met with silence. The usual quick response from the voice wasn't there. I didn't want to channel this book.

You think you don't want that because you have judgments about some of those who channel. You believe some are phonies and try to show how evolved they are by channeling.

You are right on.

The channeling mechanism doesn't correlate with how evolved someone is. Channeling is a receptive process. Spiritual and personal evolution can be either rapid or stunted in a person who channels. They are two different developmental areas. People can have high states of receptive spiritual experiences but great difficulty integrating experiences and the insights that come with them into their daily lives.

I don't want to be like that. I don't want to pretend to be something I'm not.

> Really? You already pretend to be something you're not. You pretend to be someone without a clear channel open to Divine communication with Higher dimensions. You act not to be as evolved as you are sometimes. Why do you do that?

I don't understand.

> Whatever you want to call what we are doing here— channeling, conversation, being receptive, etc. — you are doing the same thing as people who authentically channel. Why do you pretend you're not receiving a clear message from beyond your ego mind?

A rush of energy shot straight to my throat. I froze. Memories flooded my mind's eye. I could see the teenage part of me in full view.

I see myself alone under a giant oak tree at the far back corner of the schoolyard where no one ever went. I tried to pretend I was fine being alone, but I wasn't. I felt rejected and awkward. So-called friends had thought it was their responsibility to round me up and tell me how full of myself I was. I was fifteen and coming into my spiritual awakening journey, while everyone else seemed more interested in beer and marijuana. I wanted to pray and read spiritual books. I wanted to talk about higher things, but when I did, I was criticized and gossiped about. I can still feel the emotional scars.

Those scars have been with you a long time. What exactly do you feel?

My chest wants to cave in. My body wants to close in on itself in a protective manner. My breath is shallow when I remember that time in my life. I feel the tension that starts in my belly and travels up to my throat. I've done much inner work on the fear that people will think I'm arrogant, but I still feel the residue.

Do you want to know how to eliminate the remaining residue of this fear along with any other fear of judgment you have?

Absolutely.

Can we agree you don't step into the grandest vision of yourself because of an underlying fear that others will think you are full of yourself?

Yes. What can I do to burn away the residue of this fear? What's my first step?

Let the coaching begin.

Coaching?

Not only will we write this book together, but this will be a powerful coaching session for you over the next few days. It's for people who will read and benefit from our conversation in the future, but it's also for you right now. It will take courage on your part because you're not alone in this writing retreat. I might have you do and feel things you resist because other people can see and hear you. Tears might fall. The desire to scream might arise. Are you ready to surrender to this process?

Can I leave the room and go out to the beach if the urge to scream arises?

As long as you take your notebook.

Okay.

Is fear present now?

Yes.

Consider some of your exchanges with teenage friends that didn't feel good.

I'm doing that now.

Become aware of the sensations in the body. Become of the tension in your body. Where do you feel it?

I feel it in my throat down to my heart, and a little in my belly. As I feel these sensations, the thought arises, I don't want to talk about these kinds of spiritual concepts that we're writing about here and have others see it. It's not safe. However, another part of me is okay with anyone seeing this.

> Can you feel both parts in this present moment? The part of you that is scared and the part that knows this could aid and inspire others?

Yes, I feel both parts. One feels like it is stuck in my throat, and one feels expansive—more energetic than physical.

> Good, that's how it's supposed to feel. Whether the fear is stuck in someone's throat, stomach, or feet, it doesn't matter. Those sensations are the ego-self trying to protect itself from being rejected. We don't feel secure when rejected, leading to the irrational fear that we could die. One of the core fears of all humans who live in the reality of separation is the tribe will reject them, and if they are left alone, they will die. It sounds intense that the psychological self would go straight to the thought of death, but it does. Can you still feel both parts at the same time?

Yes. The constriction in my throat is still tight. The other part is light.

> Can you feel a third presence here too? The dimension of you that is aware of the frightened part and aware of the part that feels safe and okay?

Yes. I'm aware that I am aware of that.

What would you like to call these three dimensions of yourself? What feels most resonant and accurate to you?

How about the ego or protective personality, the expanded self, and pure awareness?

Nice. I like those terms.

I pause for a moment and smiled to myself. I love the lightheartedness of this voice and the love I felt coming from it. I don't perceive a fraction of judgment in any word.

Do you notice that when you focus on the part of you that is scared or think about the situation in your teenage years, you feel the fear more intensely?

Oh, yes.

Are you aware you try to lessen the intensity of your physical constriction by talking about what happened?

I feel better when I can talk to someone about something like this.

Don't talk about it. When you feel the intense need to do that, resist, without telling anyone how you feel. It's going to take you away from actually feeling the emotion.

I always thought encouraging people to discuss their challenges or feelings is helpful.

In some cases, it may be, especially with repressed emotions. Psychotherapy can help with that. Dark secrets, shame, and guilt are not healthy. Talk therapy can bring things from the unconscious to the conscious, though once aware, it's about bringing non-resistance and presence to the stuck energy so it can dissolve and end its habitual nature.

That makes sense. I can see how I keep the pain in place by retelling a story. I've always loved a little drama.

Sometimes you need to talk about something in order for the emotion and any resistance to arise in the first place—that is helpful. We want feelings to be conscious, not buried. However, talking endlessly about the repeating dynamic is not beneficial in most cases.

Can I guess when it's helpful to feel an emotion?

Go ahead.

I would feel it when it feels new. I would feel it instead of squashing it with food, alcohol, or aimlessly scrolling social media.

On the other hand, I would not touch it if it felt like I was collapsing into drama or feeling sorry for myself. I would not feel it if it felt like an old repeating pattern. Does that sound right?

You can feel a recurring older feeling as well. The distinction is this: Do not change the focus from feeling the emotion as energy in motion to talking about or dramatizing it.

I see.

> Become present to the constriction in your throat and notice what happens when I say, "You're going to publish a book that reveals that you were talking to an enlightened being, whose name you don't know, regarding your intention to become enlightened this lifetime."

When you put it like that, I freak the hell out!

> I'm not telling you to publish, and I'm not saying I'm an enlightened being. I'm doing this as an exercise. Think again about the possibility of publishing in this way.

I'm still freaking out.

> Go into the sensation of tightness and constriction. Feel it more than you want to.

I'm already there. When I go into the sensation, I start to feel sick.

> So go into it more.

Now I feel even more nauseous.

> Travel to the center of your constriction with full attention. Be in silence. Stop writing. Sense and feel.

I almost can't feel the more significant part of me that is expanded. I feel like I'm going to throw up.

> Just feel the tension. Can you bring presence or awareness to this part of your body?

Yes. I can shift my focus to the dimension of pure awareness as I sit with the tension. I now sense more of my Divine self versus my ego-self.

> Every part of you is Divine. There is nowhere the Divine is not. In a moment like now, where you experience less constriction and more receptivity, you sense Divinity. When you contract against the life force that flows through you, you'll have a lessened experience of Divinity. It's all a matter of how much one is open and receptive. The younger part, who was ostracized as a teenager, is closed down.

I think I get it.

> It's an essential concept because, without the profound realization that you are already Divine, you'll keep seeking something that you already are. Spiritual awakening is less about finding something and more about unwinding.

I love that statement. Spiritual awakening is less about finding something and more about unwinding.

When you use the word "unwind," I think of relaxing the patterns of constriction around my heart that make me need to control my mental conclusions that make me judge or feel separate. All of these stop me from experiencing my Infinite Divine essence.

> Yes, those three C words do not come to you by accident: Constriction, Control, and Conclusions. Constriction of emotion happens when the heart contracts. Controlling others, your environment, or your life force, is what happens when the gut energy contracts. Jumping to conclusions is what happens when the mind contracts.
>
> Think of it this way: if a boat on the river gets stuck in the weeds, it is not advisable to say, "Don't go near those weeds, just focus on the rest of the boat, which will somehow become freed up, and then we'll start moving again." You're already in the weeds. You must go toward the weeds and untangle the boat. Don't talk about why it got tangled or how angry you are about it becoming trapped. You separate it and move on. Move toward what gets constricted, free it, then keep flowing with the current.

I can still feel the teenage part of me that is hurt.

> That's natural. Can you honor that the teenager who feels hurt is also acceptable? She has a reaction that is normal for someone that age. Be with her with no resistance.

I will try to do that. She did the best she could at the time.

Of course she did. The unwinding process occurs organically because the spiritual awakening impulse is strong. You have to let it do its thing. Be patient, and don't resist.

I've worked with thousands of people who already know the wisdom of non-resistance, but it's not enough to bring them to the doorway of enlightenment. They need more than that, don't they?

Knowing something of that importance is wonderful, but putting knowledge into practice is an additional step. Practices and strategies can point people in the right direction. But if a person offers no resistance to what happens to them and through them, they are most of the way there.

Now, let's talk about those uncomfortable feelings of yours.

Contemplative Question:
When do you feel constriction in your energy?

Access this chapter's guided practice in the *Unshakable Inner Peace* course at: UnshakableSeries.com

CHAPTER TWELVE:
EMBODYING PRESENCE

Are you in resistance to the tension in your throat right now?

I'm less resistant than I was a minute ago.

Are you trying to fix the tension, breathe through the pressure, or do something to eliminate the anxiety?

I don't believe I am. I just notice the tension.

Good. Who is noticing the tension?

I am.

Are you aware of an observer, then?

Yes. I observe my body, thoughts, and emotions.

This observer is getting stronger in you. Very good. What else do you observe?

The sounds of the ocean. The warm weather. The clicks on my neighbor's keyboard. The tightness in my belly.

> Great. Now, transition to another dimension of awareness where you are aware that you are aware *of* the observer. Take a moment to do that.

I take a moment to feel the soft Hawaiian air against my skin and breathe a deep belly breath. I move my attention from the first dimension of awareness, the sensation in my throat, to the second dimension of observing that sensation. I then move to the third dimension of awareness, where I am aware that I am aware of the awareness of the sensation.

> Wonderful. Given that you can move your attention between the three dimensions of awareness, there is another dimension to look at. This next shift of attention I call the Dimension of Being. The awakening process is not just about knowing you are aware that you are aware of an observer who is aware of your thoughts, emotions, and sensations. It's about dropping into *Being* that awareness. In other words, embodying that awareness to the point where you have a sense that you ARE that awareness.
>
> How do you sense the difference between the following two dimensions of awareness:
>
> 1. When you know that you are aware of multi-dimensions? and
> 2. When you *Become* that awareness that is aware of the different dimensions we've talked about?

Let me take a moment to see what happens when I shift my attention from *knowing* I am aware to *Being* aware.

> Take your time. This shift into Being is what we need to stabilize as your consistent experience.

What a cool sensation I'm receiving. I'm opening, my mind goes quiet, and I feel like I'm expanding. I feel less energy and attention in my head. Now, it's throughout my body and all around me, with no mental tracking of awareness.

> That's it. That's the difference. To know that you are aware of this unconditional dimension of awareness is not enough to experience constant inner peace. It's the *Being* of it through every cell and every one of your energy centers that allows you to feel your expansive, Infinite peaceful nature. An Instagram post with a stalk of lavender and a spiritual quote that might remind you of who you are is not enough. You must *Be* it. If you don't move into the dimension of Being, the separate ego-self will pull you out of Infinite awareness and into its protective pattern again. When you stabilize this dimension of Being Infinite awareness, the separate ego-self will rarely, if ever, pull you out of Infinite Presence.

I understand what you're saying, but this is new to me. I see how I have stopped too early in my meditation practice. In my meditations, I usually track what I'm aware of and just let it go. Then I come back to observe my thoughts, feelings, and sensations. Now I see that's not back far enough.

Correct. You use the words 'back far enough' because that's what it feels like when you slide into more expanded dimensions of awareness.

It feels further back in my head and further back in my body and is wonderfully relaxing.

We will investigate this dimension of Being further, but let's return to your throat for now. Can you still feel the restriction?

Yes, but less than before.

Observe the tension rather than tell a story about why it's there. At the same time, go deeper into the tension with unconditional loving attention.

When I do, I start to feel sick again.

Good.

I have to take your word for it because it sure doesn't feel good.

As you give the tension more of your attention, what happens?

I rest my hands on my lap and close my eyes. After a few minutes of undivided attention on the tension in my throat, I find myself wondering where the tension went.

When unconditional attention flows to a place of tension, resistance is gone, and constriction dissolves.

That's what it seemed like.

You allowed yourself to experience the sensation rather than mentally observe and comment on the tension. You also didn't do anything to calm the nervous system down, which usually represses the emotion again. When there is no resistance to an experience, you are free. You can't only be in observer mode, and you can't only be in the experience. You must be in both places. If you only are the observer, at some level, there is resistance to not being in the experience. If you are only in the experience, you are not anchored in the awareness of your essential nature.

I get it. Is it that easy?

Yes and no. Sometimes, it's slight tension in the throat, but other times it's the most profound grief or anger that comes after betrayal. You must go towards and feel the emotion while knowing you are *not* the emotion. Intense emotion will shake your system more violently, so you must practice building strength and stamina to feel it without resistance.

Can you give me an example that might help me understand more fully?

Imagine you need to hold something heavy, but you can put the object down whenever you want without consequence. Then imagine lifting something heavy, but if you let the thing go, it would fall and injure someone caught underneath. In the second instance, your attention gets highly focused on your muscles so you can get stronger even though your muscles feel more pain as time lapses. If you let go of your concentrated attention on your muscles and the subtlety in your body, you could drop the heavy object. Can you imagine the amount of focus that must go into that moment?

I can.

That is the type of presence you need when you feel deep emotion and don't want to go toward it. You must go toward it as though your life depends on it. You must run towards the tiger's mouth when everything in you says to run the other way.

I've had moments where I surrendered to an emotion and arrived on the other side feeling free and clear. However, I try to reconcile how this relates to the Law of Attraction, which says that you should shift your attention from not feeling good to feeling good. Doesn't that mean I should walk away from any focus on constriction in the body, fearful thoughts, or negative emotions I experience rather than run towards it? For example, if I run toward the negative emotion, wouldn't that be just perpetuating that negative emotion?

I understand the confusion. Frankly, it confuses many. People miss how to be present with emotions in a way that allows their physical system to relax and the energetic field to open up and clear resistance. That is what moves one to a better-feeling place. Moving up the emotional scale with thoughts and behaviors that make you feel better is lovely. However, if you want to experience constant inner peace and happiness, you must ask yourself what tool you are using to move up that emotional scale to feel better? If it's drinking alcohol to feel better or going shopping to fill a void, that will not work after a few short moments. It's good to practice feeling better on purpose, but not by thinking or doing something that helps only for a fleeting moment by trying to mask the actual frequency you are vibrating at—to use the Law of Attraction vernacular.

That makes sense. Many people try to feel positive and avoid grief, sadness, or anger. No matter how much they try to put a Band-aid on something at the surface level, it doesn't shift their frequency overall. They continue to create situations that make them sad or angry. I prefer to raise my set point of joy and peace to something much higher versus just doing a thing in the moment that will have my joy meter rise and will only inevitably fall back to its original set point—if not lower.

When someone avoids feelings by drinking, eating, or watching Netflix, they may temporarily feel better, but their energetic frequency hasn't gone up. It's usually gone down because of the lack of presence that these actions can bring.

It's an ego construct to feel better in the moment because the ego's job is to avoid pain. The ego says, I want to focus on this, and then I'll be happier, or I want to do that, and then I'll be more comfortable, or in less pain. Or I'll feel better about myself.

Raising your energetic frequency is a presence thing, not an ego thing. It's a spiritual evolutionary thing. Most people think about how the ego can feel better. The great spiritual teachers of our time tell us not to try to feel a certain way by creating certain external conditions. Put another way, don't let your life's conditions dictate your feelings. You can choose how you want to feel (or choose a higher frequency idea, thought, or emotion) and follow the path of least resistance to get there. They do not say lower your frequency enough to numb out your feelings so you feel better.

It seems inevitable that some external conditions will make you feel bad even if you become an enlightened master. What unlocks the ability to feel good and peaceful almost all the time?

Multiple things need to come together. First, control where you focus your attention so the monkey mind doesn't live in the foreground of your awareness. Second, be able to live most moments where you are relaxed in the depths of your body like a soft animal when it doesn't need to defend against anything. Third, know intimately that your essence is an unconditional Infinite presence that allows your Soul to fully inhabit a human form to experience what it's like to create, play, enjoy, and awaken on Earth.

People go wrong when they translate the Law of Attraction principles using the dimension of their ego mind, which is focused on their life's conditions. The focus becomes on manifesting something they don't have to feel better after the conditions are in place. Because people usually come to the Law of Attraction principles to help them change their conditions, the focus is on attracting the relationship, the new home, the money flow, etc. The focus is less on presence and joy without any conditions needing to change. No matter how many times great teachers say, 'It's about being unconditionally joyful,' the ego mistranslates it. The focus on manifesting something can be intoxicating because it's how they think their happiness will come. They think they will be happier if they focus on manifesting something and getting it. This keeps them in a conditional, perpetually frustrated loop as they attempt to become more powerful manifestors.

I like to see myself as a good manifestor.

And so you are. But you now see that joy can't be attached to an outcome, as all effects are temporary. No matter what you do, happiness and distress will come and go, as surely as summer and winter. The resistance exists in your energy field if you're bound to an outcome.

Is trying to become a powerful manifester something I should forget if I want enlightenment?

Great question.

....

Contemplative Question:
What does the Dimension of Being feel like?

Access this chapter's guided practice in the *Unshakable Inner Peace* course at: UnshakableSeries.com

CHAPTER THIRTEEN: MANIFESTATION

Becoming a purposeful manifestor is fine. You're here to create amazing things on this Earthly plane. That just needs to be approached with caution because the focus on manifesting can be the ego's attempt to strengthen its power. The interest in manifesting can be to find happiness in something other than the essence of who you are. There is nothing wrong with a robust ego that gets what it wants. That can be a sign of maturity when things are created ethically, but it's not the gateway to inner peace. It's the gateway to becoming a powerful manifestor. A strong ego can help with many important things, like setting boundaries, feeling authentic confidence, thinking through strategic possibilities, landing your dream job, and making healthy choices. But it's not what leads to enlightenment.

The most powerful manifestation you can be part of is to experience an awakened state without anything having to change to please you. Life springs up in perfect harmony when you are in this most potent manifested state, so there is no need to intend anything.

No intentions are needed to manifest? I think you lost me.

> There is nothing you need to conjure up through your mind consciously. When you are receptive and offer no resistance to any experience, desires will naturally arise, and you'll be led through their perfect manifestation in Divine timing.

I love the sound of that.

> Here's a question for you. Can your mind make you feel better?

I believe so. I can instruct my mind to list everything I'm grateful for. I can train my mind to think positive thoughts. I've learned to switch my focus when I'm feeling down to something that helps me feel better.

> These are all helpful at times. But these mental maneuvers don't stop the underlying currents that hold tension and resistance in place, like criticizing yourself or fear of failure. You might have trained your mind to make you feel better for a while by placing its attention on a different object, but you've only dealt with the symptom and haven't dealt with the actual cause of the suffering in the first place, which is believing that your mind is you.

I believe the dominant energy I embody trumps my thoughts and words when it comes to manifesting.

That's true. You have known this for a while and live according to manifesting principles. Still, to manifest your desire for enlightenment this lifetime, I would recommend focusing less on manifesting your next goal and more on manifesting the ability to let go of control.

I think that's easier said than done.

It is, but everything in this book will help you with that. It starts with shifting your focus to your highest priority. What do you most want to manifest?

Inner peace and spiritual awakening are at the top of my list.

Everyone manifests their reality, but usually unconsciously. When that reality appears ugly, most don't like to look at their part in creating it, so they create another reality that also eventually becomes ugly, creating an unhappy endless loop.

They let life happen to them.

Exactly. Two planes of experience must be understood concerning conscious manifestation: the human (or earthly) plane, and the spiritual plane.

By conscious manifestation, do you mean manifesting on purpose through focus, positive emotion, and action?

Yes.

The first is the earthly plane of the mind, emotion, willpower, and action. It's essential to consciously wield your human powers to live a great life. The forces of communication, building something, writing, listening, imagining, and planning are all capabilities of the human being, and when you focus on excelling in those things, you will be happier.

The second is the spiritual plane of unconditional response to where you are focused. In other words, your Divine Source has no resistance to what you focus on, as everything operates within Divine perfection. Life will give back to you what you focus on. Even if you are a compassionate person but your focus is on how little money you have, you will keep coming up short.

In the enlightenment process, the mind finally recognizes your essential nature. When that happens, the mind becomes a servant to your essential nature. Your mind won't be focused on manifesting goals because you won't need anything to change to feel happy and at peace. It doesn't mean you won't want to participate in the fun play of building businesses, traveling to the places on your bucket list, and other things for enjoyment in your three-dimensional reality, but it will feel like play.

Desire seems like a massive topic.

It is a massive topic. The practical application of following one's desires is loaded with so much misunderstanding, especially with manifesting abundance and spiritual awakening. But to return to your primary question about the possibility of reaching enlightenment this lifetime, you don't need to wrap yourself around this topic now.

I'd like to come back to the topic of desire later.

Of course. The best time to come back to a conversation on manifesting desires is after you've settled into a new stage of consciousness. As you move through this gateway to unshakable inner peace, you will experience not desiring anything. You'll be in a blissful place and will want to hang out in that energy. After you ascend to this new stage of consciousness and it has stabilized in your experience for a while, you'll start to feel a natural drift back into your three-dimensional reality and will begin to experience desire again. You'll want to start to manifest on purpose once more. However, this time you'll be viewing the process of manifestation with different eyes. For now, I'll take your word for it and will look forward to discussing and understanding more.

> Notice your answers to these two questions:
> 1. What does it feel like to use willpower to change something?
> 2. What does it feel like to be in no resistance and loving acceptance of whatever occurs and know there is perfection in everything?

The first one feels hard but necessary. The second feels easy but might lead me to laziness.

The first one is more challenging than it needs to be. The second one doesn't lead to laziness. On the contrary, when you offer no resistance, there is more flow than ever, and you'll want to ride that current with a big smile and worthy goals. Laziness comes from fear and doubt, not from being in the flow.

When you only use willpower to change something, you are in an active mode rather than a receptive mode. It's OK that you create ways to think more positively. You practice not jumping to conclusions. When you start to train the thought, "Things are always working out for me," it starts to form a new neural pathway to make it easy to believe that things work out for you. This works to make you feel better. But soon enough, you'll find yourself in a dark mood with thoughts filling your mind like this isn't going to work out. This is because negative thoughts are received when your frequency lowers. A sustained frequency of joy is lived through non-resistance, not by forcing yourself to feel better.

Does this clear why pushing from willpower alone doesn't necessarily change an energy pattern in the long run?

It does. I've spent the last two decades trying to get my mind to think more positively and vision an abundant future. Still, it hasn't been enough to eradicate the deeply held pattern of fear that I will lose financial security and the fear of judgment from others. I see that upscaling my personal mindset has been valuable, but it's not led me to an unshakable presence. At least not yet.

Good evaluation. Non-resistance is the pathway to that unshakability. Non-resistance naturally raises your frequency without the need to do or change anything. This is why the way you teach how to discern one's desires is so vital. First, you must get in touch with how you feel authentically. You can allow low feelings as well as high feelings. This act of allowing puts you in the non-resistant receiving mode, which will help you discover what your heart and soul want. You can't discern what you truly want by trying to think about desires and how to get them strategically. Being strategic puts you into a limited frame of mind which can lead to falsely believing you can never get what you want. You must receive what it is that you desire, and let it come to you.

I love teaching how to discern the difference between what someone thinks they should want and what would make them feel aligned with their soul. It can be a difficult concept for people to fully grasp initially.

It's because they have been trained to use the mind to hedge what they think they can manifest rather than being in the state of allowing and receiving. Another barrier to understanding happens because giving up one's will is frightening to many. Even when one believes there is a Divine plan, it is scary to give up the ego's desire to manifest what it thinks it wants.

You are in a receptive mode right now with this book. You are receiving your desire to have your questions answered. Can you acknowledge that you have been dictating for the last few hours, letting communication from another dimension flow, and not thinking strategically about what you should be writing?

Yes, I can absolutely feel that. It's all I can do to write fast enough to keep up with you. Whoever you are. This feels amazing!

Wonderful.

But I still have so many questions. For example, what about imagination? What part does that play in manifesting a joyful or enlightened life?

There are two different forms of imagination. One type stems from human willpower, and another type comes through non-resistance and receptivity. The imagination that comes from your will starts with "I want this type of relationship, or I want that kind of home." Then it moves to the mind's eye so you can see it in your imagination. Then you might put a representation up on your vision board or write it in a journal to focus on it. It's not a wrong way to manifest as it helps you learn that when you focus the mind, you can bring things into being.

When you allow the spiritual aspect of imagination to come through, on the other hand, you will have more ease in manifesting what you want because the mind doesn't radiate its limited views of what it thinks it can create—or not. The visions and feelings that come through the spiritual type of imagination is received rather than conjured up to manifest something that the ego wants. You'll be in the middle of a meditation or walk and receive an impression or image you can see in your mind's eye.

When you're in a receptive experience, your next desire is revealed. The Divine Breadcrumbs are laid out for you. Desire is where manifestation is born. When you feel a desire, it can manifest in your Earth-plane reality.

So, where do desires come from?

At the highest level, desires come from your soul, the collective of souls you interact with, and the collective consciousness. Essentially, desires come from the interrelated nature of things. A desire feels specific to you because you play out one viewpoint of consciousness that is different from another person who plays out another perspective of consciousness, but it is all interconnected. Desires don't come from your strategic mind. This is where learning to let the strategic mind follow and serve the Spiritual Self is essential.

Freeing yourself from your strategic mind's hold is part of your last frontier. This is true for many reading this. Most of your readers already understand the importance of meditation, embodiment, and feeling their emotions in the present moment. Still, to experience liberation, they must give up the need for their strategic mind to lead their life. The ego can have a minor supportive role to ensure you are safe from a tiger and won't starve, but the ego needs to move to the background so that it doesn't cause you any more suffering.

So, it can win best-supporting actor, but it's not winning Best Director.

Ha! Yes.

To let unconditional presence lead, you need to continue to see what the ego is resistant to. Resistance towards potential negative judgments is the resistance that has shown up most consistently in our conversation so far. What would you do if you tried to make yourself feel better about your fear of judgment using your human powers?

I'd attempt to focus on something else. I could walk outside and watch the waves crashing.

In that case, you would feel better for a moment, but the fear would return when you came back inside to write. This is because thoughts are patterns you fall into.

What would you do if you didn't resist the fear and did not go outside to watch the waves?

I would walk myself through the steps I teach. First, I would start to become friends with it, and not try to push it away from my awareness. Then, I would feel it, and locate where the tension might be in my body. Finally, I would talk to that tension as though it was a part of me and find out what it needs.

Beautiful. That's why your expansion has quickened and why many say your work is the 'missing link.' You allow your fear to show itself. When you can see it, you can then use the spiritual inquiry process to see if the thought is true or if it is FEAR: False Evidence Appearing Real.

Could I use a spiritual inquiry question like, *is this thought true?*

> Yes. First, locate what you are resistant to. Then, probe into whether the thoughts are inherently true. Shine a light on your resistance.

When emotional or mental suffering occurred in my past, I can trace it back to my mind thinking about something untrue. For example, after a romantic breakup, I always thought I'd never find someone who would love me as much as I loved them. My mind constantly lied to me about this.

> It wasn't a lie per se. The ego-mind sees the world from a different dimension of reality and comments on that reality. It's the reality of a finite supply of love. It's a reality where winners and losers exist, and you must struggle to create what you want.
> When you see things from an Infinite inter-connected reality, being in a state of non-resistance and joy is easy.

When I was here in Hawaii last year, I had a euphoric experience of feeling carried by the Divine current.

> I remember.

I laid back to rest on the bed. The soft sheets moved with the breeze coming through the large glass doors I had opened as wide as possible. I closed my eyes and was transported into a boat carried by the soft current of a river. I was shown in a vision that all the results I wanted to experience were at the river's end, and the current would take me there with absolute certainty. I felt sublime relaxation as I imagined laying back in the boat while it effortlessly took me down the river to everything that I could ever want. I felt the inevitability of abundance without needing to do anything or focus on any manifestation tool. I just let the current take me. I felt more ecstasy through my body in that meditation than any other in my entire life.

> That's it. It's as easy as that. However, this is where many Law of Attraction students get stuck, as they don't listen to the most critical parts. They keep coming back to thoughts like, "I want more financial abundance, a better job, my perfect relationship, or home." All of that is already at the river's end, where they will arrive if they let go of resistance. The irony is that's not even where happiness and fulfillment reside. Joy is the experience of receptivity in the moment. The purpose of human life is joy and well-being and creating from an Infinite vantage point, but the ego doesn't see that. It feels like its job is not to let go of those paddles and push against the current all day long.

My mind often thinks it's got to be more complex than that. That I have to make enough money to survive. That I have to work hard and be responsible. Right now, it's thinking that I can't just get in a boat and be carried down a beautiful, peaceful river for the rest of my life.

Therein lies the challenge of you becoming enlightened in this lifetime. Your mind is working with your ego to keep you safe, but it can't see the big picture. Are you willing to get into the boat, drop the oars, and relax?

I am. I want that, but I know it will take practice.

Think of it less as practice and more about awareness of when you surrender to the current and when you don't. You are more surrendered right now. You can tell because you feel better. The corners of your mouth are turned up as you type, and you feel more flow and life force. Right now, you are in no resistance to the process.

I feel so light at this moment. I'm breathing deeper with a happy heart.

Do you remember what happened a month after you had that beautiful meditation of the boat floating down the river? What did you manifest more quickly than you could ever have imagined?

....

Contemplative Question:
Is there anything you would prefer to manifest than unshakable inner peace and happiness?

Access this chapter's guided practice in the *Unshakable Inner Peace* course at: UnshakableSeries.com

CHAPTER FOURTEEN: MIRACLES

Datta and I had a decade-long dream of living on a piece of land with great views just outside of town. We are introverts who love nature, quiet, and lots of space. A few days after my ecstatic "boat in the current meditation," we flew to Australia for five weeks.

During my stay at my family home, I had the idea, more than once, to look into a property that could combine our home with an office for our work team. I received the idea that if we let go of our leased office, we would have the cash flow to pay a higher mortgage for a home with a great workspace. I emailed Eric, our realtor, to let him know of my idea and to see if there were properties in our Northern Colorado area that would be zoned for what we wanted. I wanted to be integrity with his time, so I told him we'd probably need years to figure out financing given a larger property would require a sizable down payment and higher monthly payment. Eric replied that he would investigate. My mind flooded with ideas daily on how a new space for our home/office on acreage could work. Could we build from scratch if we couldn't find an existing home we wanted? Maybe we could have a house, office space, and a retreat room to hold some of our smaller events?

I became obsessed with looking at eco-friendly building options online. I envisioned a rammed-earth structure that we could build from scratch. I investigated architects who made homes from shipping containers. I designed our new shipping container home on scratch paper, which made my family laugh. Apparently, the thought of living inside a shipping container was hilarious to them, since they all knew how much of a princess I am.

Giggles morphed into hysterical laughter when I told my family about buying vacant farmland and building from scratch. Datta and I could live out of a trailer for a year or two, I told them. As a woman who felt the cold more than anyone they knew, they couldn't see me in the middle of a Colorado winter in a trailer.

Still, the dream of our new place lit me up with excitement. From Australia, we flew to Japan for events we presented at a gorgeous retreat center with a view of Mt Fuji. I took photos of natural wood beams on the ceilings, beautiful entrances, exquisite decks—and anything else architectural I was attracted to.

Finding suitable land that would be zoned for everything we wanted was a long shot. Even if we found the right property, there would be a lot of pieces that would have to fall into place. We would need a deposit for the right architect, the down payment, construction loans, selling our existing house, and subleasing our office, to name a few. I got an email from Eric, our realtor, two days before we left Japan. He said he'd been looking at options and wanted to show us a few of them and talk more about our vision so that we could formulate a plan.

Though there was no real urgency, the excitement in my heart took center stage, and we agreed to meet the day after we got back from our international trip. It was all I could think about.

Eric sat in front of us on the couch of our office foyer and said, "I think I've found the perfect place for you."

"Wow! That was fast, though we're not sure how fast we can do this, given our current finances," I reminded him.

"That's fine. Let's follow the leads we have and see where it goes. I went to have a look at this place myself earlier this week. Then I took my wife because she knows you both, and we thought it felt like the two of you."

He handed us the most organized, color-coded binder I'd ever seen and flipped it open to the page for the property he spoke of.

That weekend we visited a 35-acre property with views of Pikes Peak and other mountains in the Rocky Mountain National Park, with massive unique rock formations on the property itself. A hundred trees surrounded the home, and a streaming water feature ran through the backyard to die for.

Eric couldn't get the front door open at first, forcing us to walk around the grounds for a while before entering the house. I couldn't believe where I was and what I was looking at. It was breathtaking. We didn't know 35-acre properties existed that close to town. One of the best things about it was that two ridges separated it from town, eliminating a hundred percent of all traffic noise. The effect was magical, from the moment we stepped out of the car.

I hoped I would like the house and would at the very least get some ideas about what whatever house we found or built could be like. The layout of the interior couldn't have been more perfect. It had a separate entrance to the office space and a large walk-out basement. Both areas would be perfect for the team. Datta and I would have our privacy in the main home area. We loved it. We knew that one day when we could afford it, we would get a property just like this.

On the ride back home, we were all excited but reminded Eric that it was way out of our price range.

"The first step is to call your mortgage broker and see what they say," Eric said. "Don't give up yet."

Still doubtful, I called our mortgage broker that afternoon to see what we could qualify for. She surprised me, saying we would qualify for a loan on that property. All we needed was the down payment. Through conversations with her and investing-savvy friends, we realized we had a lot more equity in our home than we'd believed initially, as well as an unexpected return on an old investment.

Within days we put in an offer on the house. Datta suggested we should offer more than they were asking, which sounded crazy, but I finally agreed. After a few more tense days, our offer was accepted. We found out later that the sellers had received a full-price immediate cash offer they would have taken had we not offered a few thousand over the asking price. It amazed us how it all came together as if by divine arrangement, which is why we named our home Miracle Hill.

It's a powerful and emotional memory for you.

It is, because if we can manifest that, we can manifest anything.

It wasn't all smooth sailing after that, though.

That's an understatement. Our loans got hung up, and we almost lost the deal twice. Our trusted realtor told us on three different occasions that the deal probably wouldn't go through, and we might as well give up. We had to keep giving the sellers more earnest money to extend the contract. Ultimately, through willpower, hours of diligent work, and our strategic minds being 100% focused on that sale, it all worked out, and we moved to Miracle Hill a few months later. It saves us money each month, and we are building equity in a home and office that makes us feel blessed and abundant every day.

I want you to understand it's less about your willpower and concentration on what you want to create next and more about being in the flow of receiving ideas, joyful feelings, and having fun on the journey.

So where does action come into the picture of manifesting a joyful life? Some might ask, "Do you mean I should just let go and not take action?"

That question only arises because people want a black-and-white answer with no paradox in sight. As I've said, there's a difference between action that comes from human willpower and action that comes from receptivity as you follow the divine breadcrumbs. When you get an impulse to go this way, say this, or say that, if you're in non-resistance, you will receive that impulse to move and take action. You will trust and go. If you resist, you put the brakes on and complain about how much hard work it will be.

When you use your imagination from human willpower, you do it from a limited vantage point. On the other hand, your spiritual self can send you impressions, insights, and plans that can shorten the perceived distance to manifesting what you want. For example, when you finally stopped imagining the type of man you thought you would like to be with, you instead asked the perfect question: "How do I want to feel around my perfect man?"

As soon as you asked that, you received an image of a goofy man who came up to your window and pushed his nose against the glass to make you laugh. This image was received through imagination. When you imagined your perfect man from a small vantage point, you always pictured Tom Selleck, but we won't hold that against you.

I hear you laughing at me.

I'm laughing with you. It's pretty funny, and even funnier when you consider how well Datta fits that image of the goofy guy outside your window.

I guess I've always had something for eccentric men who are older than me.

What other impulses, images, or ideas have come to you that you felt were received?

The impression of combining the home and office was received. I didn't consciously conjure that up. Earlier in my life, I remember seeing myself in an auditorium, a beautiful old theater where I stood before many. I thought I was singing, but I might have been speaking. That vision has come back to me many times.

It's good practice to notice which images you receive spiritually and which you direct with your mind because you think they will make you happy. Notice how you feel differently in each.

Let me check in with that and see if I can feel the difference.

Take your time. These distinctions are important.

When I conjure up something and try to keep my mind focused on it, I experience doubt that it can happen. Something is triggered in my psyche to make me fear it won't happen. I feel attached to it happening as I believe it will reflect on me poorly if I don't manifest it.

When the image is received, it feels like a gift, and there is no doubt. My attention stays focused on receiving it instead of me trying to be a great manifestor. There is less attachment, and more natural curiosity and excitement.

The second kind of imagination comes from an Infinite vantage point. You can trust it more.

I believe that.

....

Contemplative Question:
What's the difference in your experience between receiving an image or idea versus directing your mind to focus on an image and idea?

Access this chapter's guided practice in the *Unshakable Inner Peace* course at: UnshakableSeries.com

CHAPTER FIFTEEN:
LIVING IN DIVINE FLOW

I have a question that's been bugging me: If I get in the boat to be carried by the Divine current, do I never have to meditate or control my monkey mind? Can I just do nothing and float, and I'll eventually be enlightened? I can't imagine you mean everyone is enlightened, and we're just not admitting it to ourselves.

Once again, we must ask the question from different vantage points: your human and spiritual vantage points. Your spiritual nature is Infinite and unconditional. There is nothing ever that needed to happen for it to awaken. It does not look to be enlightened. It does not need to meditate. It already floats and receives.

Your human ego-persona holds on to the idea that the mind and body are who you are. The more you sense that your mind and body are you, the more it stops you from experiencing your essential spiritual nature. To not fall into its traps, it is incredibly beneficial to meditate and have some control over the ego-mind's monkey-like nature. Your ego also doesn't need to do anything to be enlightened. It never gets enlightened. The ego needs to be seen through so another dimension of seeing can take its place.

Thank you for making that clear.

> The choice is to get into the boat and receive the current that supports you. You can always jump in and take the ride, or you can decline. Think of peace, freedom, happiness, and unconditional love, as things you experience in the boat when you float down the river.

I picture a scene in my mind's eye.

> I put it there for you. What do you see?

I'm walking across a large grassy area and see a river ahead. I see a small boat with oars tied up to a small pier.

> As you approach the banks of the river, imagine you have a choice to get into the boat or not.

I'm walking towards the boat and would like to get in.

> Someone greets you at the edge of the river's bank and warns you not to get in.

I see a man in a guard's uniform. He says, "There are rocky rapids around the corner. It looks peaceful now, but it gets dangerous down there. You might get badly hurt or even die, so please don't get into the boat."

You listen to that guard at the water's edge. He gives some pretty serious reasons about why you shouldn't get into the boat.

I would presume they know more than me about what is around the river's bend and that they have my best interest at heart.

> That guard represents how the ego works, constantly trying to protect the status quo. It tries to keep you alive and away from the unknown or what is risky.

I often hear this warning voice as if it has my best interest at heart, but it's just my ego.

> The ego gets a bad rap. It has a job to do, and helps you to belong, feel loved, and keep safe. However, it cannot see from the spiritual vantage point that you already belong, are loved, and are safe. You are the nature of belonging, so how can you not belong? You are the nature of love itself. You are already safe because your essence is safety. It doesn't know this because it operates only through the body's psychological self and feelings. It's your ego that is the guard at the side of the river. That ego-guard is willed solid because you've never been in this boat before. You've never fully let yourself be carried. You've never trusted long enough to feel the bliss and ease of being always carried to where you want to go, so you listen to the guard, who has a powerful voice.

There isn't anyone in the boat. It's empty and rocking gently in the water.

> It unconditionally waits for you. It doesn't mind if you get in or don't.

Intuitively, I sense it would be great to get in and that the boat will take me somewhere beautiful, but I don't hear a voice saying, "Get in! There's nothing to worry about." All I hear is the guard's voice in my ear, emphatically saying, "Don't get in!"

> Which voice do you believe?

My choice is between a guard who sounds like they know what they're talking about and an intuitive pull toward an empty wooden boat. I lean toward believing the guard in this circumstance and suspect most people would do the same.

> Yes, and that's the problem. If you believe the guard, you will not get in the boat. As soon as you get in and relax with the current, you will more readily feel your essential peaceful and joyful nature. It's as easy as that.

My heart opens when you describe the energy of being carried. In my imagination, I'm on the boat. I feel the moment expand into timelessness. I feel my happiness meter go through the roof. I guess the key is not to believe the guard. If I'm right, what is the best way to do this?

Not believing the guard is one way to get into the flow of the current. Another option is to get in the boat when the guard is not looking. That means feeling what it's like to float down the river and be carried by the current when your mind isn't so fearful. The more your mind can trust this experience of being held, the more it won't be so strong in its warning to not get into the boat in the first place. You've had experiences of being carried by the current, haven't you?

I have.

Tell me about some of those experiences.

Writing my last book, *Divine Breadcrumbs,* was one. Upon arrival at the writing retreat, I thought I would write a how-to book for people who want to make a greater impact in the world. After the opening meditation, I was met with a vision of my mum, who had prematurely passed away a couple of years prior, and heavy tears fell down my face. She was my muse that guided me to write stories I had forgotten. The more I wrote, the more I surrendered to the flow. Because of that choice, it was a magical experience. I chose to give up my intellectual will to experience more mystery. It anchored a new, spiritually deep message I am supposed to share but have often held back.

Finding and buying Miracle Hill was another of that kind of experience. Any time I have surrendered and allowed the spiritual vantage point part of me to take over, it's turned out more powerfully and beautifully than I thought possible.

When I first moved to America in 2002, I moved to Ashland,

Oregon, instead of one of the bigger cities I originally thought would be a good fit. I initially had cities like San Francisco, Austin, Chicago, Nashville, and New York at the top of my list. Every morning for a year, I chanted my mantra: Guide me, protect me, and I will follow through. I was open to following the flow of where I was supposed to be, but I couldn't see a clear answer from my strategic mind's standpoint until I was invited to visit Ashland. A town of 20,000 people became the best spiritual college I could've asked for, and it's where I met the most significant gift of my life, Datta.

> Wonderful examples. They have helped you build your surrender muscles. The more you know the beauty of being carried down the river to places and experiences that are better than you imagined, the more you will laugh at the guard at the side of the water.

This conversation about stepping into the boat to be carried has put me in a higher state of receptivity.

> I see that. As you stay in this receptive state, imagine going past the guard on your way to the boat, who is shouting, "Don't get into that boat! There are rapids and rocks! There is possible injury and even death around the corner. Whatever you do, *do not* get into that boat."

I can feel his intensity.

> See the boat in the background, tied to a pole waiting for you. How do you respond?

The guard's warning would affect my mind on a low self-esteem day. But right now, I feel great, so I find myself giggling at the guard. I tell him, "It's okay. I'm willing to take my chances. Thanks for caring." I don't try to convince the guard that I'll be fine. I smile, knowing they will never know how magical that current is. I don't have to change the guard's role, or resist the guard, teach the guard, convince him that I will be fine, or make him go away. Instead, I don't spend any time with the guard. I move on with no resistance.

> What if the guard reaches out and grabs your hand and pulls you to the ground?

Yikes, would the guard do that?

> Yes. Sometimes to them, it's life and death that you do not get on that boat. It's their job to protect you, so they will do whatever it takes if they are scared enough for your safety. If your ego, a.k.a "the guard," has got you cornered or pinned to the floor, you must realize at that moment if you fight back, you are not going anywhere. You must stay in non-resistance. Tell the guard, "Okay, I won't fight you." Be with him and tell him you hear him and will stay with him. If you fight kicking and screaming, you will lose your energy. You've got to become an Aikido master with your ego-guard.

How do I eventually get into the boat?

Simple. Slip on by when the guard is not looking, which happens when he doesn't have to be so on guard. When the guard enjoys the water's edge and gets distracted, move on and get into the boat. Have you heard it said that you cannot move from frustration to joy in an instant?

Yes, I've heard that in different ways.

This relates to how the guard feels. If he or she is angry, you can't just say "I want to move into the bliss boat." But when there is joy in the guard's eyes, you will have little resistance to getting into the boat.

When you learn to be more receptive, the guard relaxes. When you're having a great day, that's the time to do something you've wanted to do that's previously been scary.

I see.

The guard is sneaky, though, and tries to get you to think, "I will only get in the boat if it leads me to where I want to go." The guard usually wins because you are focused on what will bring a particular outcome versus being receptive to seeing where the current takes you as you enjoy life.

What you just said is huge.

I know. Unfortunately, most people miss it.

I don't want to miss the hugeness of this.

> You won't.

My limited mind thinks that if I get into the boat, the expansion of my career will cease. I'm very focused on growth and my capacity to create right now.

> That focus is fine, but can you feel the difference between being naturally drawn into expansion versus wanting to make it happen so you can manifest more?

I can. But if I'm honest, I get scared when I consider letting go of control and letting the boat carry me.

> Scared of what?

For one thing, scared that I'll become boring.

> You've hit a pocket of resistance, that's all. Shine your light on it. If you don't, the guard will continue to say, "If you get in the boat, you will become boring." But that's not true.

What the guard says to me feels true. Especially when memory supports his words with evidence.

> That's what the ego does. It supports its warning with memory as evidence. What memory surfaces for you right now?

I'm at a dinner party with friends, in my mid-twenties. I had recently read a spiritual book on silence and that night tried to practice what I'd learned. I sat back in my chair, centered myself, and listened. I kept quiet. After a while, my best friend turned to me with a scrunched-up nose and asked, "Why are you being so boring?" Maybe she was a half-kidding, but . . .

I bet that hurt.

It did. It really stung. Later, when no one else was around, we cleaned up the kitchen, she asked me, "What's going on with you?"

"Nothing," I responded. "I've noticed how sometimes I'm not present instead of listening to people, so I was practicing the opposite of that."

Then the famously dreaded words came, the ones I'd heard many times before. "It comes across like you think you're so much better than the rest of us."

I dropped my head and continued washing dishes in the warm soapy water.

Memories get wired into the system of the protective psychological self, to give our ego-guards the proof they need to create compelling arguments.

I'm ready to give up my defenses and am prepared to meet anything head-on.

When you surrender and get into the boat, your capacity grows because you become one with the current. You are no longer a person battling your mind. The current that runs through every living being is much stronger than your ego, mind, or heart. Would you agree?

Definitely.

So why are you not going with the current?

I have no idea at this moment, and I'm laughing at myself. It sounds stupid not to go with the current.

You said earlier your focus is on your capacity and growth. To do what?

To lead more effectively, make an impact on more lives, and become more creative and less stressed by all the things on my plate every day. I want to expand my intuitive capacity and my ability to manifest the perfect opportunities for my career to grow. I also want to expand my capacity to love and not be so reactive to other people's challenges and triggers.

Then ask yourself this: If I switch over and let the current carry me, which is as powerful as the entire Universe, will I have a greater capacity for all these things?

When you put it like that, it seems silly to even ask myself. Of course, I'll have a much larger capacity. Extraordinary amount of capacity. It would blow my mind.

In ways you can't yet imagine. Your mind would be bobbing above the water somewhere else while you are enjoying the peace and bliss of floating down the river.

I'm ready for that.

I can tell because you are receiving these words in the river right now. You can feel it. You don't know where this book will take you, but you receive guidance and inspiration and have little resistance to me.

Are you going to tell me who you are?

I already told you I would, but not right now. It would incite too much resistance in you.

My head wants to know who you are so I can put things into greater context. I want to ensure my image to the reader isn't tarnished. I want to ensure you are not some archangel with a weird name so you don't ruin my reputation as a down-to-earth gal.

That is your ego-guard speaking. You hear its voice but are getting into the boat anyway. Once in the boat doesn't mean you will stay there. Your ego can convince you to get out, which is fine because it gives you a chance to get back in. Be ready for a lot of practice at this.

Everyone's guard defends differently. I know you love the Enneagram as a psycho-spiritual tool, so consider nine ways the guard can protect against relaxing into the Divine current. I'll share a story with you to illustrate my point.

....

Contemplative Question:
In what ways does your ego-guard warn you?

Access this chapter's guided practice in the *Unshakable Inner Peace* course at: UnshakableSeries.com

CHAPTER SIXTEEN: THE NINE GUARDS

I'd love to know more about the ego-guard, and how to get past him. Or is it a her?

> It's neither really, but it can appear as either. That ego-guard can be very tricky, having been created by your own mind and intelligence to keep you safe. It learns new and more effective tricks all the time to stay in control. The greatest trick of all is to make you think your ego is you, and that its voice, in reality, is *your* voice.

That's a bit of a mind-bender.

> It is. Your ego has had lots of time to position itself as your ultimate authority. An authority you have become accustomed to obeying.
>
> Imagine walking up to the edge of a river where you are met by someone who looks like they are there to help you get into the boat. With a big, trusting smile, you declare, "I'd like to get into that boat as I have heard that it is a magical boat that takes you to places that only a few people can see. I'm so excited about the journey."

A stern look appears on their face and they say, "It might take you somewhere nice, but there is a right way to steer this boat and a wrong way to steer this boat. If you don't do it correctly and instead make mistakes, you could get into serious trouble. You could smash the boat, which will upset the owner and you will owe a lot of money to get it replaced. You could seriously hurt yourself or drown. If you are not 100% positive you can steer this boat perfectly in rough conditions, then you should not get in until you've had time to practice in easier waters."

That sounds like the Enneagram Type One's predicament: to avoid making mistakes and to do things perfectly, stopping them from entering the flow of life.

The Enneagram is a good model for understanding the ego-guard, especially since you understand it so well.

Thank you. In the past, I've stopped surrendering to the Divine current of life due to fear of not doing things perfectly. I don't want to make costly mistakes or get others upset with me if I do something the wrong way.

The Enneagram Type One is called "The Perfectionist" for a reason. Each Enneagram type has its own mental habits that stop them from entering or staying in Divine flow.

What are the mental/ego habits of the Enneagram Type Two, "The Giver"?

This time, the guard at the boat says, "Yes, this might take you somewhere nice, but others need you here on shore. Your family and friends need you, particularly those struggling with major issues in life. Wouldn't it be selfish if you left them behind and just did this for your pleasure? What would they do without you looking after them and being there when they really need it?"

I can relate to this one as well.

It's important to remember that everyone has a little of each of the nine Enneagram types, but a lot of at least one type.

I have stopped surrendering to the current of life because I didn't want to be selfish. I knew people counted on me, and my duty to others has traditionally taken precedence over my own desires.

Let's try another scenario. This time, the ego-guard says, "Sure, this boat might take you somewhere nice, but what if you fail at this journey? Everyone knows you are attempting this journey, and everyone will see you fail. You will almost certainly not get the successful outcome you want from this mission. At least on the shore, you can keep achieving the success you have because you already know the rules of the game, and you usually win. There is a new set of rules you don't understand on the river and stages along the journey where you could fail. Think of all the things you won't be able to do while in the boat. Most of the time, you won't have anything to do."

Once again, I can relate. Enneagram Type Three is called "The Achiever." It wants to be the best and succeed in the eyes of others and is always busy doing a million things. What about my favorite, Enneagram Type Four, "The Romantic?"

> Yes, this is your primary type. A look of concern appears on the guard's face and they say, "Sure, this boat might take you somewhere nice, but you will have to let go of all the extraordinary things you want to manifest and release all the deep connections you have with others. Your closest relationships will move on without you and have wonderful lives while you are stuck on the boat on your own. Surely you don't want that. You might think the ride will be amazing, but it won't lead you to some idyllic end. There is no incredible finish to the ride. There is much more to enjoy and connect with here on the bank."

I can see my addiction to wanting to move toward what is extraordinary and will lead me to a spiritually idyllic end. This is definitely my go-to ego-guard. How does the guard manifest for Enneagram Type Five, "The Observer?"

> This time, the guard shakes her head and says, "Yes, it might take you somewhere nice, but there is no way to know *where* it will take you. We should sit down first, learn about the journey, and get all our questions answered because if you don't know how this journey unfolds, it will put you in an unsafe predicament. Then you don't have to even go. After all, learning about a journey is sometimes better than

being on it. Remember, the unknown and being away from your own protected space brings up anxiety in you, so you won't be able to enjoy the journey. You don't want to be in anxiety, do you?"

This is less like me.

Right again. But it is also just a little bit like you. We all have parts of all nine types, as I mentioned before. Denying any of those parts can also be a maneuver on the part of the ego.

Tricks within tricks! Tell me about Enneagram Type Six, "The Loyal Skeptic."

In this scenario, the guard frowns and says, "This boat could possibly take you somewhere nice, but there are many dangers you will need to mitigate. You probably won't even make it to the end. Many don't survive the trip. You wouldn't believe all the bad things that will probably happen if you got into the boat. You might hit the sides of the banks and get stuck, and no one would be there to help you. You could hit rapids, fall out, knock your head on a rock, and drown. Let's sit down first and go through all the worst things that could happen, so you are prepared, because some of them will almost certainly happen."

I know many who would be met by that kind of guard. Tell me about Enneagram Type Seven, "The Enthusiast."

This guard frowns at you and says, "This boat might take you somewhere nice, but it might also take you somewhere painful. You'll be alone. The majority of the ride is not fun. It might appear like an adventure, but it isn't. It's a long, boring day, just sitting in the boat doing nothing. When you get a great idea, you'll be unable to act on it and will feel limited in the boat. You won't be able to get out of the boat for months or years. You won't have many options to keep things interesting, and with little to do or think about, the experience will get stale fast. I'm sure you will feel boxed in after a while."

Yikes. That doesn't sound very attractive.

None of these scenarios do. That's the job of the ego-guard. They know their person well and know exactly what arguments to use to be as convincing as possible.

Can you tell them about Enneagram Type Eight, "The Protector?"

Of course. This time they say, "This boat might take you somewhere nice, but you are bound to lose control at some point, and you'll be put in a vulnerable position. You'll feel weaker than you ever have against the huge rapids. The rapids are a lot stronger than you are. More importantly, once you are on the boat, you cannot protect those in your life. They'll be left alone on the banks to fend for themselves. If you don't survive, everyone will see that you couldn't be the strong one after all. People on the banks will see you and laugh at your weakness. Do not get in the boat if you want to feel like you are in control and a powerful protector. It's just not worth it."

I know Datta will relate to that.

I won't tell him you said that.

He already knows.

Yes, he does.

The last Enneagram Type, as you know, is Type Nine, "The Peacemaker." This time, the guard says, "This might take you somewhere nice, but more likely, it will be the most chaotic and unbalanced ride you'll ever take. It looks calm and peaceful from where we're standing, but rapids around the next bend go on forever.

Plus, you will upset the harmony of your life that you have worked so hard to create. People will be angry at you if you take this ride and don't consider them. They rely on you. Have you considered everything and everyone? Why don't you stay with the lovely, harmonious life you are already in?

When you get into this boat, the journey will be anything but peaceful. If you love chaos and the feeling of being unsafe, get in. But I don't think that's you. If you don't want to be totally off-balance, then just stay here on the bank. You can thank me later."

The guard has many strategies.

> Indeed! The guard will do whatever it needs to maintain the status quo and has lots of practice learning how to successfully manipulate you—all in the name of keeping you safe. At times it will seek variety but will only allow a small amount of metered unpredictability.
>
> The moment when most spiritually inclined people halt their progress is right before surrender occurs. It happens right before the last step into the boat. Most will love the quiet of the boat (emptying the mind), and the peace in the body that comes with being taken by the current. Still, to give up on the unknown of what is around the bend is very difficult. Which of the nine guards stop you or concern you the most, Rachael Jayne?

For me, it would be 3, 4, or 7. For my husband, it would be 7 and 8.

> Very good. It's helpful to know how your particular guard operates. That way, you can recognize it working and see through it. Your ego doesn't want you to surrender to the current of Life. It wants to remain in control. The journey of spiritual awakening is unwinding the control, contractions, and conclusions that keep the guard tightly wound and trying to protect you. Your higher self wants to take the reins, but the guard doesn't want to let go.

I want to be carried. I want to be in the current.

Then that needs to be your highest intention. You need to stop sacrificing what is great for what is good—maybe even extremely good. Whatever takes priority in your life *becomes* your life. Being on the river is an analogy of being in the experience of receptivity. The Divine current runs through you. The more you open yourself to receive the Divine current, the more you will experience the spiritual dimension you ultimately want.

....

Contemplative Question:
Which of the nine guards stops you the most?

Access this chapter's guided practice in the *Unshakable Inner Peace* course at: UnshakableSeries.com

CHAPTER SEVENTEEN: QUESTIONING ASSUMPTIONS

I feel ready to untie the boat, get in, and let the current take me. I can't help thinking it's pretty safe for me to take this ride given I have a secure marriage, a beautiful home, a fulfilling career, and supportive friends. I'm blessed with the luxury of time and space for self-realization, which many are not. People could say, "Rachael Jayne, it's easy for you to sail down the river, but I have to keep two jobs to feed my family." I can understand where they are coming from.

You have as much to lose as anyone else, if not more.

I guess I could lose my home, which has happened before. I could lose a lot of money paying for the work team I can't afford anymore, which has happened before. I could lose friendships, which has happened before. I could lose my health again.

The argument that it's easier for you does not stand up. Over centuries monks, meditators, and spiritual teachers had held this stage of awakening when they didn't have riches or a lot of support. They had small means, but they prioritized learning how to get past their guard and into the boat. You received the current of the Divine when you didn't have much to your name.

You may be right. I immigrated to the USA with one suitcase and my underwear stuffed in my guitar because I didn't have the money to upgrade to a second piece of luggage. I didn't own much, but was in the flow of following my dreams and listening to spiritual guidance. When I finally got to a point of making enough money to not just survive, I went through years with a back injury and couldn't work. I could hardly move, let alone do what I needed to bring money in. I needed at least $3,000 per month to cover expenses and stay in the USA rather than return to Australia. I asked for Divine support and received directions on who to call and who to ask for promotional help so I could fill my first coaching program. I had no time to listen to the guard. I had to do something fast to stay in the country I loved.

> So, when you get in the Divine current that feeds the entire universe, do you not think that your needs will be taken care of?

On one hand, I get it, but the other part of me thinks I'll end up losing everything. I'm concerned about losing our business if I surrender to Divine will.

> That is the guard's voice in your ear. A few minutes ago you were saying how you were ready to get into the boat. You see how this works?

I'm beginning to.

> Here are two questions to ask yourself. Write down the answers you get.

Question #1: What will happen if I become wildly successful in my career?

Question #2: What will happen if I fail in my career?

I hate the word, "fail."

I know you do.

I stand up, bend over to stretch my sides, and watch the waves break for a few minutes. I love being away from my usual surroundings. It forces me to be more receptive to the moment, and takes me out of my routine. I feel a quieter-than-usual presence inside me.

I sit down and type the first question. "What will happen if I become wildly successful in my career?"

The answers come quickly. I have to type faster to keep up.

- *I will have less time off.*
- *I will have more money to invest in things I care about.*
- *I will be on the road more of the time.*
- *I will have a larger team and more help.*
- *I could be more overwhelmed by the amount that is going on.*
- *It would be easier to get clients.*
- *I will need to get better at saying no and having better boundaries.*

I look at my list and pause. They are not all good, but are not all bad, either. I move to the second question. "What will happen if I fail in my career?"

- *I will feel disappointed.*
- *I will not be able to hire more help.*
- *I will be stressed about money often.*
- *I will have to do things I don't want to do.*
- *I won't be able to purchase the items I want.*
- *I won't be able to spend as much time on things I enjoy, like writing.*

This list is all negative, none of which I want.

> Now that you have a start on both lists—because there are more points to both you can add—are your answers so far true? For example, take your first statement, that if you become wildly successful in your career, you will have less time off. Is that actually true?

I assume it's true.

> Right. It's an assumption, but not inherently true. Take your next answer. "I will have more money to invest in things I care about." Is that true?

Yes.

> Are you sure?

Yes, because I will have more money coming from my successes.

That might be partially true, but doesn't building a wildly successful business take much money to build?

Sure. It costs a lot to run a business.

Is it possible that you wouldn't have any more profit in your bank account even if your career takes off?

I guess so, but my sense is that won't happen.

Isn't it possible that you could have a wildly successful career, but something happens with your or your husband's health, and you'll have to spend a lot of money on health care? Couldn't something else happen that would suck your money from you so you cannot invest in things you care about?

I hate to think about that, but anything is possible.

When you ask whether it is true, is it 100% reliably accurate?

When you put it like that, having more money to invest in what I want is not inherently true. I don't know what could happen.

Is anything on your list true?

I think the one that is most likely true is that I'll be disappointed if my career doesn't go well.

You mean if you fail. But is that actually true, or is it that guard that told you "everyone will see you fail"?

It feels true.

I know it *feels* true, but *is* it true?

I guess something else could take its place that makes me happy or arrive at a point where my emotions are not affected by my level of success or failure.

Your spiritual path will guide you to a place where you can't be disappointed anymore.

That sounds great. I'd love to be in that place.

You can't be disappointed when you know and embody the real you. When someone knows who they are, they see through the illusion of disappointment.

Disappointment has been my friend for a long time.

I asked you to make a list of beliefs around success and so-called failure because your mind concludes what will happen by creating assumptions drawn from past experiences and its limited vantage point. You must question these assumptions. Even if your career is a failure, you might be left an enormous inheritance from a great auntie you never knew you had. Or you could create income from some other source.

That's true. There could be other sources.

> When you investigate the truth of what your mind tells you,
> you'll find that not much is inherently true. When you shine
> light on the truth, you can see how the mind works to make
> assumptions, and how unreliable the mind is.
> It's making things up constantly. It doesn't even know what
> is true or not. Sitting in the mental state of not-knowing is a
> powerful practice. Being curious relaxes the contraction of
> the mind. Being in a receptive body also relaxes the mind's
> contraction.

When I relax the contraction around my heart, I focus on softening the edges around my heart's energy center. Should I do the same around the head energy center? Would that ease the knee-jerk pattern of mental conclusions?

> It would. Do you want to do that now?

I would.

> Close your eyes and bring your attention to the internal
> space of your head. Locate the center point of your head
> along the vertical core. When you are there, soften the
> edges around the center point and your skull. Notice what
> you experience.

It takes me a few seconds to do what the voice instructed. I locate the center of my head and soften my focus. My mind instantly goes quiet.

No thoughts. No commentary. It's like turning the lights off in a messy room of a hoarder, then turning them on in a clean, orderly room. I sit for several minutes in sublime silence.

I feel a rhythmic pulsing through much of my vertical core. It's as though I can feel my heartbeat in the center of my head and the center of my solar plexus. The more I focus my attention inward to the center point of my head, the more expanded I feel. It's counter-intuitive, but I experience myself getting bigger.

Do you feel more receptive?

Absolutely! I feel incredibly open. I feel no defense.

This is because there is no constriction now around your head center. When this happens, the mind can't assume or conclude. By softening the edges around your head, you can remain in the state of not knowing.

The quiet is stunning.

This is your essential nature.

I never want to leave this space.

You will, trust me. There'll be times when you'll want your strategic mind to work on things. What you want is to be able to return to this dimension of Being at will, anytime. To do that, you must know with certainty that this dimension of stunning quiet is always present. It doesn't come and go. It's unwavering in its presence. It's you that comes and goes.

My mind hasn't been unwavering in its presence up until now. It gets busy and then slows down at times.

That is your mind. This essential presence has always been and will forever be unwavering. You just haven't had your attention pointed in its direction much.

I hear you yet again remind me that it is not the mind that I need to quieten. It's about pointing my focus to a different dimension.

That's right. This is sinking in.

I'm not always the fastest student, but I'm committed when necessary.

Your commitment is one of your greatest assets.

That's what Datta tells me.

He knows you well.

It's break time at the retreat, but I don't want to move from my seat as I fear losing the energy of this glorious moment. I need to pee, though.

Then you can practice non-attachment to any state while on the toilet.

Why didn't I think of that? What a perfect place to practice non-attachment and letting go.

> You see, when you are in the receptive flow state, you are hilarious. Now go pee. And practice coming back to this state in every situation, while doing any activity.

Contemplative Question:
Is that thought true?

Access this chapter's guided practice in the *Unshakable Inner Peace* course at: UnshakableSeries.com

CHAPTER EIGHTEEN: MOUTH OF THE TIGER

Can we talk about non-attachment for a moment?

Of course.

There are definitely things I'm attached to.

Whatever you are attached to creates resistance and stunts your ability to receive. Attachment occurs when you think, "If this happens, I'll be happy, and if it doesn't, I won't." There is fear built into attachment. Attachment stops you from a direct experience of the present moment. Instead, you seek for something to happen in the future or grasp onto what you have. This is why working to loosen attachments is vital on the spiritual awakening journey.

I feel the truth of that.

What are you most attached to these days?

Our beautiful new home.

What else are you attached to?

I want creative freedom in my business. I only want to work on projects I'm excited about. To cover the mortgage for Miracle Hill, I need to make sure money flows in. I can't always do what I want because we won't hit our income goals if I don't work in certain ways for long hours.

> Then you also need to let go of the attachment to how you make money.

I know money can flow through positive intent, but I also believe it's created through hard work and focus. I work with many clients who don't do what is needed to make their business work. They don't do enough marketing, which leads to not enough sales. They don't learn to write compelling copy or share their message enough. Are you saying those skills are unimportant in building a financially successful business?

> No. I'm not saying that someone who wants to be a world-class musician can succeed without an instrument and lots of practice. You can't become a first-chair violinist without serious effort. It's the same with business. You can't succeed without the instruments of trade, like marketing, hiring, and cash flow projections. It's not worthwhile for us to argue about action or non-action. It's a matter of whether you allow the Infinite dimension of you to take the lead and let human effort and action be its faithful servant. At the height of Albert Einstein's career, did he lead first with intuition, curiosity, and receptivity to ideas or did he lead first with traditional science and

mathematics? Did JK Rowling lead with curiosity and receptivity to ideas when writing the first Harry Potter book, or did she lead with a left-brain strategy to outline the best-selling fantasy novel of all time?
I think you know the answers.

I do. It was the first scenario in both cases.

Think of a person you consider awakened that you have listened to or watched recently.

Eckhart Tolle comes to mind.

Okay. Did Eckhart sit down and write his books, or did he get in the boat to float and do nothing?

He sat down and wrote them.

Spiritual teachers actively share their message. They don't just float on their guru chair and do nothing.
Let's get back to the central issue here of non-attachment. Another word for attachment is resistance. Attachment happens when you worry about losing or missing out on something. For example, you might believe you could lose a level of happiness or freedom, but your true nature is already happiness and freedom. Can you see that being attached to something points your focus away from your essential nature?

I think so. One way that helps me let go of attachment is to remind myself to be less specific with what I want and open to what's in my highest interest. I've had enough experiences to confirm what I initially thought I wanted was contrary to my best outcome. I learned that in romantic relationships. It hurt when I got attached to someone, hoping they would be my life partner.

> It slowed things down, didn't it?

Yes, it did. I was energetically tied to one guy for two years. It wasn't working out and didn't fulfill me, but I thought it was as good as it probably gets, so I was attached to him being the one.

> You pushed against the current, and that's why you were depressed about that situation for such a long time.

I didn't want to get stuck there ever again.

> Then don't get attached to anything having to be a certain way. It's fun to receive intuitive impulses and plan to make them happen. Just don't get caught thinking something must happen. Can you feel the freedom in going for what you want but not caring if you get it?

I suppose I could be in a consistent state of not caring about the outcome. That would be freeing. I believe things would flow at a quicker pace, as well. When I let go of attachment, things happen better than I imagined. I go in and out of non-attachment. How do I remain in it?

The best thing to do is rest your awareness in the eternal moment of now. Have a direct experience of being present. Make love to the present moment. Receive the moment. Attachment is only created when you feel that the present moment is not enough, which puts you in the seeking mind.

How do I make love to the present moment?

Feel so aligned with the present moment that you *become* the present moment. When you are in a receptive state, you can do this. When you surrender your mind, relax your body, and open your energy centers, you can experience the eternal moment. It's how it is when you make love to your husband, and every bit as remarkable—but more so because it is available to you every minute of every day. Plus, you can do it in public.

That's funny. Is there anything else I can do to let go of my attachments?

There are practices you can do for the long-term relaxation of all your attachments, and there are practices you can do when you catch yourself feeling the stress of attachment. Let's start with a practice you can immediately institute regarding your attachment to keeping your beautiful home. It begins with thinking of the worst things that could happen if you have no money to keep your home and lose everything.

That sounds pretty scary.

Call this practice "Walking into the Tiger's mouth."

Are you serious? You sure know how to relax a woman.

> I'm not here to relax you. Now that we have that straight, what's the first thing you would need to do if you had no money to keep your home?

I would have to alert the bank and tell those closest to me that we must move and why. It would be humiliating. My stomach sinks just thinking about it.

> Then what would happen?

We would have to sell furniture, pack our belongings, and try to find somewhere else to live.

> What would you do if you didn't have enough money to rent elsewhere? This might happen because you can't sell your home in a down market, or you sold it for a significant loss.

I'd have to find a friend to take us in.

> What would be the worst thing about that?

Our failure would be widely known. Everyone would remember that we boasted about our Miracle Hill adventure, and how we manifested this amazing and beautiful place. Then a few years later, we get kicked out because we had no money. People would either judge us or feel sorry for us—or both. I couldn't stand that.

But if it happened, would you be okay?

My self-esteem would take a serious hit, but Datta and I would be okay. We would find a way to start again. Ultimately, if we have each other, we can be happy anywhere.

Which is exactly what happened when you lost your home and left Oregon. Can you see how looking directly at the worst possibility loosens the attachment to it never occurring?

If I take a few deep breaths and contemplate whether we'd be okay if this happened, the answer is yes. I just have to switch my focus from the worst reaction I might have if this terrible thing happened to the truth that I would be okay no matter what.

Now, close your eyes and see if there is an even worse possible scenario.

The scene appeared quickly.
I see myself driving down our long driveway with just my car full of stuff and my tail between my legs. Datta has left me because I was so irresponsible with our investments. I'm forced to go to the next-door neighbor because no friend wants to take my dog and me in for months until I get my act together. I knock on the neighbor's door, utterly humiliated, with nowhere else to turn.

If this happened, would you be okay?

No. I mean, eventually, I'd be okay. I have figured out enough solutions to big problems, so I'm sure I could do it again. I can imagine looking out the window of my neighbor's spare bedroom to the property I loved and now lost, knowing that this too shall pass.

> Take a moment to feel that "okay-ness." Feel that even if the worst thing happened, you could move on.

I drop my fingers from the keyboard and recognize this realization that I will always be okay has to settle into my body for it to land as truth. Belly breathing helps. Feeling the essence of my heart helps. These things remind me that I am in the present moment, and I can make the next move when I am present. I'm never stuck.

If I dare to go toward what I'm most afraid of, I can look into that Tiger's mouth and see that it's not that frightening.

> This practice is like playing chicken with your ego. If you keep peering into what the ego is trying to make you fearful about while you continue to ground in the truth that you are undamageable, you win the game of chicken, and the ego gives up and chickens out.

I love that idea. Playing chicken with my ego!

> You can use this practice on anything, not just your home. In the short term, if you notice the stress of attachment at any given moment, you can take a few deep breaths, sense

your vertical core, and lean back into the back half of your body. Leaning back is a physical movement that signals the brain that it's safe to stop grasping so tightly. The body feels and then sends a signal to the brain. You can use this to your advantage. Alter your posture, add a smile, or feel the internal space of your legs and how strong they are. Whatever physical cue you choose, it can make you feel less attached.

Remember, non-attachment is freedom. It's the freedom that comes when you are open to all possibilities.

It's hard when my mind continually concludes what is possible and can't be achieved.

That's your ego-guard, doing its job. When you put your head center in a state of receptivity, curiosity is imperative. Otherwise, the mind goes into problem-solving mode. You can disengage the mind that thinks there is a problem that must be solved in two ways.

1. See through the illusion of the mind with the question, *Is this true?* After sitting with that question, it will take you into receptivity.
2. Be more receptive by softening the edges of your head center, which will quiet the mind.

Either way, what do these two choices lead you to?

Receptivity!

Exactly! When you are receptive, you are free of attachment at that moment. Imagine what happens when you've practiced being receptive so much that it is your default state.

No attachments would arise to pull me out of presence. My mind wouldn't engage in controlling or problem-solving.

Being in the receiving mode walks you through the door to inner peace.
Pause and ask, what happens when your mind doesn't have a problem to solve?

I stop writing for a moment and contemplate a life where there are no problems to solve. I feel the furrows between my brows deepening. I'm confused.
No problems to solve? Then what do I do?

Tell the mind to do nothing.

I close my eyes. Mind, you can do nothing.
My mind is blank with no response.

Well, that is a sign of a better-trained mind than most. Most minds would immediately rebel because the mind's job is to solve a problem to improve the present moment.
What's your mind's first rebuttal when you declare there are no problems to fix?

There might not be any problems right now, but there will be one later. You'll see.

> Clever mind. It's making sure that you don't discard it for good. Like the ego, it is tricky—and neither even knows that.

There are, of course, problems that need to be solved. People have to pay bills, look after the kids, get through an illness, or fix their relationship issues.

> You can always give your mind a job, but you must watch its addiction to believing there is a problem.

What if I turn into a hippie singing "Don't worry, about a thing, 'cause every little thing is gonna be alright," along with Bob Marley?

> What would be wrong with that?

I hear my husband's voice saying, "If you're going to hang out in Hippyville and not help fix the problems we face, I will have to fix them."

> Has he ever said that to you?

No.

> Has he ever said anything like that?

Not exactly, no.

> Yet your ego-guard says he might.

I guess.

> You guess right. How many problems has Datta brought to
> you that aren't problems?

The ones he brings up are manageable but must be dealt with.
Otherwise, they could get out of hand. For example, if an employee
keeps making too many mistakes, he would say it is a problem. It
seems like a problem to me too. I can't just sweep issues under the
carpet and expect my husband to handle it all.

> To have a spontaneous reaction with presence in any
> situation is acceptable. In this case, a spontaneous response
> would be to talk to the staff member and ask what needs
> to be in place for the mistakes not to occur again. When
> someone judges it as a problem, it becomes emotional and
> gets a hold on them, so they are no longer in the flow. You
> will see people try to prove that you must get out of the
> river's current to fix what they think are problems.

I don't want to get out of the flow for anyone anymore.

> Receiving the Divine current doesn't mean you don't act on
> things you want to change. You want to partner with life,
> not retreat from it. You have the current on your side, so

take the action you're inspired to fix the so-called problem, which really isn't a problem. I can imagine you working on solving something while singing, "Don't worry about a thing, 'cause every little thing is gonna be alright."

I giggle and sing Bob Marley's song to myself.

You have a lovely voice, Rachael Jayne.

Thank you.

Did you work on your voice?

Yes, though I suspect you already knew that.

I did. How many hours did you spend on singing lessons and practicing your voice?

That's hard to say. I would guess between 15,000 and 20,000 hours before I got to where I wanted to be with this skill. I also taught voice lessons for six years, strengthening my vocal ability and practice.

Well, mastering the spiritual arts that open someone to the experience of enlightenment is no different.

What are spiritual arts?

There is a trilogy of practices that are central to this development.

What are they?

....

Contemplative Question:
What does non-attachment mean to me?

Access this chapter's guided practice in the *Unshakable Inner Peace* course at: UnshakableSeries.com

CHAPTER NINETEEN: UNSHAKABLE TRANSFORMATION

If someone has a sincere intention for spiritual awakening, they need to work on three developmental areas that ease the identification with the body-mind. The sooner they can work on all three simultaneously, the more progress will be made. If you can find a spiritual teacher who does all three—which is rare—then you've hit the jackpot. You teach all three, which is why many of your clients say your work is exceptional.

Earlier in our conversation, you said something to the effect that multiple things must come together for someone to move from being a relatively happy human to becoming a fully awakened being. Are these the three areas you speak of?

Yes.

I take a moment to look back through my notes.

You said, "First, control where you place your attention so the monkey mind doesn't live on automatically in the foreground of your awareness. Second, be able to live most moments where you are relaxed in the depths of your body like a soft animal when it doesn't need to defend against anything. Third, know intimately that your essence is unconditioned Infinite consciousness that allows your Soul to inhabit a human form to experience what it's like to create, play, enjoy, and awaken on Earth."

After re-reading that passage last night, I felt you gave me the Universe in one paragraph.

> I was pointing towards the trilogy of practices that train the Earth Suit to experience enlightenment. Remember, it's not the Earth Suit or the person that gets enlightened. The Earth suit becomes receptive enough to have an unwavering experience of your essential nature, so it doesn't believe you are a personal ego anymore.
>
> The good news is you have progressed far into your mastery of this trilogy. You've already bathed yourself in these three important developmental areas, creating an easier path to get past the guard and into the river's current for good.

Can I try to expand on those three areas?

Of course. Give it your best shot.

Well, I would say the first would be understanding one's psychological and personality structure to be able to stop identifying with it. When I started to see how mine operates in finer detail, it was easier to create space between my mental habits and the self-aware observer.

Spiritual teachers often say, "Don't identify with the ego." That's hard to do because the body-mind instrument has made it feel like your personality, body, and ego are you.

Who else would I be if I were not the person called Rachael Jayne Groover?

> That will be unveiled. It's an embodied realization that will clarify who and what you are. It won't come from me explaining your essential nature in different words than I've already given you. It's through this trilogy of practices that it will be unveiled. Remember, spiritual awakening is more about unwinding something than finding something. You will have this embodied realization when you loosen the habits that have kept you bound. This trilogy of practices helps the unwinding process.

The second part is somatic awareness. This would include embodiment practices to stay anchored and relaxed in the body when uncomfortable emotions arise, which helps to not identify with the body and its emotions.

> Exactly what is your definition of somatic awareness?

Somatic awareness happens when you focus on internal physical perception and experience. When you survey your interior physical space and listen for signals your body sends about pain or constriction, you can loosen and unwind existing patterns that have kept you limited. Focusing on body awareness and physical habits can open one's energetic capacity and develop more conscious ways of being.

Correct.

The third part of the trilogy is spiritual practice. You have helped me understand that spiritual practices, when done as intended, are practices of receptivity. Authentic prayer makes one receptive. Meditation makes one receptive. Forgiveness makes one receptive. Sensing a Divine Presence that is greater than oneself makes one receptive. Spirituality is its own developmental area that connects you to something greater than your small self.

> Good expansion on the Trilogy. There are many practices and paths, but these are the three most important areas of development.

I'd like to hear more about this trilogy.

> Personality is built on mental habits, emotional habits, and defense mechanisms. At times the personality is expressed with positive attributes and at other times with challenging ones. When you observe your psychological patterns with presence, it starts to relax the focus on being a separate self with an identity to protect. Your personality is not going away. You won't become boring with no personality. In fact, the opposite will happen. You will have more love pouring through your being, which allows more of the nature of your soul to shine through, rather than the problematic traits of your ego-personality.

My mental habits have been to focus on what I don't have versus what I do have. My mind has droned on for decades about everything missing in my life that everyone else seemingly has. My mind has concluded that I'm somehow flawed and will never have what I want most.

I was reading a journal recently I wrote back in 1999. I was blabbering about how my best friend had found her soul mate, and I asked my journal in a classic twenty-something entitled way, *"What has she done that I've not done? It's so unfair."*

My emotional habits nicely dovetail with the "Woe is Me" drama I've perfected over time. I've often felt shame that I am different and don't have the life others have. Then like the flick of a coin, it turns into pride that I am somehow more unique and memorable than others because of this difference.

I also see my habits of envy, disappointment, and feelings of never being fully satisfied. If I have times of happiness, I expect them to be extraordinarily high, which I can get too often. But soon after an ecstatic period, there's a depression around the corner. My best friend growing up called me the "troughs and peaks gal." I had no idea what she was talking about at the time, but I laugh nowadays, because I see that pattern in high definition.

One of my primary defense mechanisms has been fantasizing about ideal experiences or relationships and believing I should also experience that perfect level. This is a setup for always being in the seeking mind and constantly feeling the grass is always greener somewhere other than in my ordinary life.

Learning the intricate movements of my personality has been assisted through understanding the Enneagram and daily self-reflection. The time invested has given me the vision to see my ingrained habits enough not to follow them with knee-jerk unconscious behaviors. A psychological pattern would appear when I was younger, and I'd be off and running with all my energy following that. Now I have a choice that makes me less defensive and opens me up to higher frequencies of my personality, specifically joy, compassion, and serenity.

All of this was in my blind spot years ago. It had to be shown to me, and then I needed years of looking for these patterns to be more conscious of them. I can't say they are now gone without a trace, but I at least am aware of these patterns and can honestly say they affect me far less than they used to.

Are most of the mental and emotional patterns people wrestle with in their blind spot?

> Yes. It's why this first leg of the chair—seeing your psychology at play—is critical for awakening from the illusion that you are your ego.

What are other examples of dysfunctional psychological structures we might be able to recognize in ourselves?

> The mental habit of judging that there is a right way and a wrong way to be can quickly turn into righteous anger and repression of positive, natural impulses.
>
> The mental habit that says you must give to others to receive the love and attention you want is another example. Even if this means sacrificing your needs and desires, it can turn into a negative emotion of pride. Deep down, you believe you are indispensable because you do so much for others. Focusing on what could harm one's safety and security can

quickly cement more habits of doubt, fear, and believing in catastrophic imaginings.

Continuing to keep the peace when you really want to stand up for yourself and ask for what you want.

Reining in these habits is a significant job, so they don't run our lives.

Having self-control over mental, emotional, and physical habits comes first in the path to spiritual awakening. You must tame the beast of the monkey mind and unwind the kinks in the energetic hose so emotions can flow more easily and don't get stuck as habits. Otherwise, when you have a blissful experience of the Infinite dimension, it will be easy for life to kick you back to the ego world, and you'll wonder why you lost that awakened feeling.

Going back and forward between the experience of Infinite peace and the unsatisfied ego is the ping-pong match I'm stuck in these days.

It's crucial for you to understand that it's okay to do that. Probably the most important thing you are doing in that context is being aware of what side of the net the ping-pong ball is on. If you tell yourself that it's not okay to ever be on the ego side of the net, it will ultimately create great resistance to being where you want to be.

The word "current" continues to be an excellent word for this part of our conversation. A current runs through your body. The more it's allowed to move uninhibited, the easier it is to stay present in the Infinite dimension and connected to the idea you are not your mind, body, or personality. To get into the boat to be taken by the river's current is one thing, but to remain in that current everyday life takes experiencing the current through your body as a normal experience. The Divine current you receive through your body sometimes moves freely, and sometimes it's pinched off through being resistant or attached, but it's always present.

I think that is why somatic practices are so important. Twelve years ago, I became fascinated with the presence inside my body, particularly the subtle core energy that moves through us from root to crown. The more refined my awareness became of my vertical core, the more present I felt, and the more presence I believe I transmitted.

You were also drawn to Dahn Yoga and Tantric Dance simultaneously, so something wise was moving you in the right direction. Yoga, dance, and various forms of martial arts are where others find their way into this world of somatics. Still, some people practicing somatics get stuck with a primary focus, like manifesting the perfect stance or a tight butt in their active wear. versus tracking the internal space of the body with more precision.

With an abundance of cellulite from an early age, I knew I wasn't destined to have my dream butt—with or without leggings. Maybe my rear end was a Divine gift because it made me rigorously focus on my internal space. At least I could get good at that. This somatic awareness enabled me to witness my emotions and triggers rather than fall prey to them. It allowed me to relax rather than follow that tension with defensive behavior. It alerted me early on when something didn't feel aligned with my higher self.

Do you see how somatic practices have helped you to not identify with your body and its emotions and sensations?

I hadn't thought of it like that, but I believe you are right. Attention to somatics has been a game changer for me.

The capacity for somatic awareness pays off big time when you hit the biggest pockets of resistance that keep the doors closed to enlightenment. When you sense resistance, you'll feel closure in the internal space of your body. You'll feel your heart or gut constrict. You'll have more of those experiences soon enough. When you do, you must find the balance between two seemingly opposing stances.

1. Put focused loving attention on the tension in your internal space. Move awareness toward the constriction.

2. Don't calm the nervous system down. When you calm your system, numb feelings, or try to breathe the tension away, you shut down the power of releasing the energy that wants to come up and out to unwind old patterns. Some people constantly try to calm their system through moving toward comfortable things. That only keeps the usual habits in place.

I'm not sure if I know how to strike this balance. They seem like opposing forces.

> Don't worry. You will when the time comes. By staying focused on the tension, you'll breathe, stay in your body, and soften around the edges, but you won't try to repress anything, suppress anything, calm yourself down, or try to stop the emotion that wants to come up and out.

I presume feeling more receptive in moments of resistance would be helpful too.

> Always. Spirituality equals receptivity, and vice-versa.

Can you explain more about that?

> Spirituality is the practice of letting go and experiencing the unconditional presence of the Divine. Spirituality is the practice of receiving this Divine love, which courses through your human instrument to be expressed and experienced here on Earth.
> Does that make sense?

It does.

> Which of the three developmental areas have you mainly focused on up until now?

First, it was psychology. Twenty years ago, when I was first interested in spirituality, my practices were mostly about trying to understand and control my mind. Then my focus moved to the body and understanding emotions. More serious spiritual practices like meditation came in later. Do all people go in the same direction and order?

> No. Some might follow the same pattern as you, but people choose different places to start, depending on the mentor who shows up when they are ready.
> Some begin with yoga and, in turn, the body's connection to Spirit. Some start with shamanism and the relationship to nature and the spirit world. Some begin with psychotherapy. Some with meditation. Some develop their spirituality through organized religion. It's okay to start with the most comfortable one and go from there. There is no race to enlightenment, and there is no need for it.

No need for it? Why am I doing this, then?

> Before you get your panties in a twist, hear this. Everything continues to evolve and expand. Humans, animals, and the planet will continually grow in awareness and manifestations. To be more accurate, it's through understanding that everything expands. When someone becomes more conscious, desires and other ideas are birthed out of that consciousness. If you don't consciously intend to expand, you will still grow.

How is that possible?

You will experience challenges and celebrations to help you become more conscious of your desires. Through pain or pleasure, you will expand. If it's not in this life, it will be in another.

Most people have not yet fully decided that enlightenment is within their reach, so they don't have it as a vision for their life. This is unfortunate because it is attainable. It's simpler than most think. Not easy, but simpler. People tend to complicate the spiritual path and put other things higher on their priority list.

Spiritual awakening is at the top of my priority list. The potency of my New Year's Day intention was undeniable. I'm going for it. I think I will tell Datta about my writing experience this next break. It's been amazing communing with you, and I feel a lot more confident to share what I'm writing about with him. I've kept it close to the chest until now, but I think I'm ready to share that you have shown up for me, and we're writing this book together.

You ask great questions, Rachael Jayne.

I'm glad you think so. I've got plenty more brewing.

Contemplative Question:
Which of these three areas of development have you focused on the most?

Access this chapter's guided practice in the *Unshakable Inner Peace* course at: UnshakableSeries.com

CHAPTER TWENTY: CHALLENGED

I just told Datta what my book was about, and it brought me back to five months ago when I told him I decided I was going to focus on enlightenment in this lifetime.

That was a test, wasn't it?

It sure was. I told him I heard a clear voice that wasn't my own. I shared how you and I were conversing about the enlightenment process and that I felt like the book was more for me than anyone else. Before any words of support, he fired off his usual challenging comments. "If it's only for you, why would anyone want to read it? How do you know if the voice is telling the truth?"

When I shared with him how you said it would be easier for more people to experience enlightenment in the future, he also challenged that notion.

I could scream if I didn't have such a knot in my throat right now. I'm triggered. I know he's a challenger, but jeez, can't he first be a little happy for me and this experience I'm having with you, or at least pretend?

Maybe he is happy for you, but that's just the way he's conditioned to respond. You did say that was usual for him, and that he's a challenger.

But why did he have to do that? He'll say things simply to challenge what I say, especially regarding spiritual matters.

> Like you said, he's a challenger. You may not be able to change that. You can change how you react when he challenges you, though.

I notice my desire to talk to someone about what just happened so I can have someone on my side and get reassurance that I should continue to write this book. The pull is strong to determine what others think of what just happened to back me up, but I will resist the temptation.

> That's a good call on your part.

I feel if I talked to someone else, it would be a way to disperse the charge of emotion and get into mental storytelling. Something you said earlier makes me think I should be present with this trigger for a little longer to explore it.

> Who's feeling the insecurity that arose with your husband's remarks?

My ego.

> Can you feel the constant presence of your essential nature even though you're triggered?

I need a minute for that. Let me check in with my body.

Checking in with your body is good, as it's the best way to see if you are in a mental, emotional, or defense mechanism pattern of the ego-personality. Where do you feel the closure or constriction in your body?

I feel it in my heart. I have just shared something risky and now feel vulnerable and shaky. Datta should know better. When someone first shares the kernel of their new creative baby, he shouldn't come in with his bulldozer questions and squash the idea so soon.

Understandably, you want him to behave differently, but unshakable inner peace will only come when you do not blame Datta—or anyone else—for your upset. Instead, let what created the disturbance in the first place be something that can momentarily pass through your experience without judgment. If you can, it will unwind itself, so it doesn't have to continue its knee-jerk-conditioned pattern. You have kept that pattern in place as soon as you judge, think, or process it.

I don't mean to be harsh about this, but your upset is happening 100% because of your resistance to what Datta said. He's not the cause of your upset.

What do I do to never get upset at him again when he challenges me before saying something nice, especially when I feel vulnerable, like sharing about a new book I'm writing? I can't imagine you mean that I should just put up with it.

No, I don't mean just put up with it. Don't learn to be a

doormat. But you can do many things to train your body and mind to not get triggered by the same thing over and over. You could choose one aspect of the trilogy we just spoke about: Psychology, Somatics, or Spirituality.

One. You could recognize that your upset is your psychological pattern and witness it for what it is. The essence of you is not upset.

Two. You could move your attention to the constricted place in your body and invite the body to soften its edges with somatic awareness.

Three. You could become more receptive or sense the dimension of your Infinite awareness and rest your attention there.

These are great suggestions. I want to be able not to get upset no matter how intense my husband is at any moment.

That's a worthy goal, but dear Rachael Jayne, stop and take a breath.

Realize you're doing something with me that most people wouldn't understand. Datta receives powerful insight in his own way but doesn't receive it in the way you do, and when he's triggered by something he hears, he challenges before he realizes he's doing it. You have a way of receiving insight and breaking things down into practices that can help people make tangible progress toward inner peace and consistent well-being. You're masterful at that.

Tears well in my eyes as I hear your sweet reassurance. Should I take a moment to feel the emotion that is coming up? It's not anger, and it's not fear, but tears are present nonetheless.

Yes, take a moment to be with that energy in motion.

As I sit with the tender emotion and don't label it or try to tell a story that justifies it, I feel more buzzing in my arms and hands.

As you breathe into these sensations, along with the constriction in your heart, find a balance between being present with the core of these sensations and being aware of the feeling of spaciousness in the body. When you stay present to the spaciousness in and around the body, it's easier to stay anchored in presence while not suppressing feelings. When you remain in this state, your mind can't run away with the story of why you are right, and Datta is wrong.

As I put my attention on the spaciousness in and around me, it feels good. To feel more spacious, I focus on the inner space of my body. I imagine softening the edges of my body and becoming more aware of the energy field around me.

Stay with the sensations and spaciousness a little longer, then tell me what happens next.

As I take a deep breath and sink my back more deeply into my chair, I hear voices and laughter wafting in from outside. Waves crash. A slight breeze kisses my neck under my hair, which is pinned up due to the heat. I feel more stillness. Less churn of thoughts and emotions. I'm not latching on to the story of "he said this, and I said that." I'm so used to my mind re-running interactions and making him wrong for saying this or that and myself bad for reacting a certain way. It's nice to feel that pattern of my mind subsides on its own.

> Can you now feel the part of you that never moves, even if the ego is upset? In other words, can you feel the eternal presence of your Being that remains still?

Yes, I can. The more I don't do anything with the emotion but make space in my body, I feel my breath again and can feel that stillness and equilibrium come back into my present awareness.

> Feel into that constant stillness and presence.

It's wonderful. I don't feel reactive anymore. With your guidance, I understand that if I didn't go toward the sensations or emotions, my thoughts might sit there and stew. At the same time, I'm not stirring up any emotion or thought by processing or talking about what happened, I'm just letting them be, and in turn, they unwind on their own.

> Awesome.

This reminds me of the days I'm stressed, and all I want to do is cry, but I try not to. Finally, something happens where there's too much tension built up because I don't allow myself to cry. I let the tears out and feel better. That kind of release is not full of story or complaining.

It's just a physical and emotional letting go.

> The reason why you feel better after the tears is because you release resistance. Don't clench down on the energy that wants to move through you. Allow it.
> Notice now what eyes you see with.

I'm seeing with my non-judgmental eyes. I see more clearly.

> That's right. Breathe into the stillness you feel.

I noticed a fearful thought that just arose in my mind.

> No problem. Thoughts pop. What was it?

It's the fear that I'm married to someone who is unconsciously trying to sabotage my spiritual growth, and he doesn't want me to work on elevating my consciousness in ways that he disagrees with. What do I do with that fear?

> That fear comes from your ego. The fear comes from your history that people will not appreciate you if you become a tall poppy. You know this pattern, don't you?

I do. It combines with the fear that I will outgrow someone and abandon an important relationship when I don't want to, or I'll be rejected because someone judges me as arrogant.

Repeat the same thing we just did before. You become aware of the fear. Is it your essential nature of still presence that feels this fear?

No, it's a part of me that doesn't want my husband challenging my spiritual experiences.

You love Datta.

With all my heart.

On a scale of zero to ten, with ten being someone who challenges every single little thing and zero being someone who doesn't challenge anything, what number would you give Datta?

I think about this before I respond that I would give him a seven or an eight.

Can you be more precise?

Okay, I guess I would give him a 7.5 on that scale.

That sounds about right. Now, if I handed you a magic wand, and you had the power to change anyone's challenge level with that, would you make Datta a two or a three on that scale?

Oh, no. Some push-back is good. Just not too much.

> Got it. What if you could make him a five on that scale? Right in the middle between challenging everything and challenging nothing.

That might be okay.

> That *might* be okay?

Yes, it would be something I could live with.

> So why not be okay if he was a two or a three on that scale?

Because if there's wasn't enough challenge, not only would life and our relationship not be as interesting, it would be harder to stretch for my goals. I just don't want too much challenge.

> So you've said. You've also said five on that scale would be "okay," and you could "live with it." Not very enthusiastic response. What if he was a six on that scale? Would that be ideal?

I think so.

> Your ideal is now one and a half points from where you said Datta is on the challenge scale. Is the difference a matter of comfort?

Maybe. I think for a moment. Probably. But even though this makes sense, I still fear the fear I mentioned before.

> Observe that fear. Don't go into a story of what happened in the past or what might happen in the future. The past would sound like "he always does this," and going into the future would sound like "he may never change."

I feel frustrated. Am I going to have to put up with him challenging everything you and I discuss in this book just because some of it opposes his assumptions?

> That's you going into the future, my dear. It's okay that fear arises, but if you go into the past or future about it, it sticks to you.
>
> He might challenge something on every page, but your goal is to be present and watch the emotions and the thoughts that rise and fall. What if those challenges help you create a better book that will impact more lives?

Why can't he help me without the big challenges?

> Are you asking why can't he just be someone else?

No, but I don't think it's too much to ask for this minor adjustment.

> For him to make that change, it may be too much to ask. But if you want to live in a state of awakening, you must reconcile that this is not about him. It's about

you. The pebbles in your shoe keep you from being unconditional and present. The awakening journey is to know and remove those pebbles. Everything I'm showing you here is about how to remove them. Many people's biggest pebble in their shoe is their significant other, so don't feel so special with this issue. Significant others tend to bring up things that wouldn't come to the surface any other way. Otherwise, we'd have to call them insignificant others.

That's funny.

> You are okay with many of the ways *he* reacts and is triggered by *you*, but here is a place where you cannot remain still.
> You change how you see any situation by the eyes you choose to see with. Your ego eyes make up a story about how the other person is wrong. When you see through the eyes of the Divine presence, you see everything in its proper perfection.

I'm getting an a-ha as I come back to presence. The fear is not so much about being challenged. It's about being left alone and that I'll have to publish this book without his full support. It's my core fear of abandonment again.

> Beautiful awareness. Let's look back to the same practice we did earlier, but at a deeper level of presence. Let me walk you through it again.

Step 1. Observe the fear. In this case, it's fear of abandonment. He has always been your biggest supporter and will be with this book too, but at least for now, something has triggered you into feeling abandoned. Step 2. Feel the contraction in your body. Where is the emotion stuck in your body?

This one feels more in my gut. It's like I've been punched in the stomach.

With unconditional presence, put your attention on your gut center while you sense spaciousness around you. Don't resist being in that tense area, even if it makes you feel queasy.

Step 3. Blow up the fear in your mind to see the threads of thoughts that create the fear. Your threads include: Datta is not going to support me, he's not going to understand why we're having this conversation, I won't feel safe talking to him about our process, he doesn't get me spiritually. Am I close to the contents that move through your mind?

You are right on the money.

I'm sure you feel emotions that stem from these thoughts.

I want to curl myself up in a ball and hide.

Then do that. Curl up and welcome the sense of contraction. No resistance.

Step 4. Don't disengage from feeling your emotions until the constriction in your gut loosens on its own. Don't tell a story about the emotion. Don't do anything to calm it down. Just Be. When you sense it calms down, feel your breath again and notice the natural expansion because your life force freed up.

You can do other things if the constriction doesn't free up on its own. For example, you can talk to the fear and use specific breathing patterns, but the most important thing to do is feel the experience and name it, but don't tell a story about it. Feel it in your body with no resistance, and rest in the unwavering presence of the Divine that is always there.

As I take those steps, I feel more settled.

You just projected a whole bunch of stuff on Datta. Your mind believes he's done things in the past to make you think he might not change. That's not true. Most relationships are just one projection after another. You have lessened your projections over the years, and you see Datta with the eyes of presence and love most of the time, but you weren't there today.

I see that now. It feels terrible when I don't see him through the lens of non-judgment. Do I say something to him? How do I know when to leave it because it's something that I have to deal with, and how do I know when it would be helpful to talk about?

Each moment and situation is different. There is no wrong choice about whether you talk to him or not. Take the theme we've been on about non-resistance. Don't resist the urge to share with or not share with him. Notice the urge that arises and ask yourself which part of you has the urge. Is it your ego that says "I should talk to him; otherwise, I won't feel okay"? Or is it the spontaneous moment saying, "I think it would be good to have this conversation, and I'm not attached to how it unfolds or resolves"?

This can be slippery. Datta and I don't like to sweep things under the carpet.

There's no need to talk about everything that triggers you if it was a passing experience and you're not holding on to it. That is a focus on the past. Focus on now and what feels unresolved now. Situations between the two of you are not swept under the carpet if they don't affect you anymore. When you are in a state of flow with a client, you gather insights about the person. There comes a time when you choose whether to say something to them about your understanding. There's no right or wrong choice. Instead, you feel the impulse, check whether it's coming from ego or essence, and choose.

That's easier to do with clients and harder to do with an intimate partner. With clients, I check in with my attachment to their response to what I share with them. If I notice I'm attached to looking wise or being right, I don't say anything at that moment because my ego is in the lead.

Use the same practice with Datta. You have more attachments in your marriage, but this is where the most significant work to your enlightenment will happen. It's much easier to hold the state of non-reactivity when you're alone, but you have chosen this relationship with Datta for your spiritual growth, and you have chosen an intense character to practice with.

Good thing he's handsome and a good kisser.

So I've noticed. More importantly, take a moment to check if you have any attachments about how Datta responds to your sharing about how you felt during your last interaction with him.

I do. I have an attachment that he hears me, gets me, and doesn't challenge me with a harsh tone in his voice again.

Then I suggest talking to him when you feel less attached to his response. That doesn't mean you sweep it under the carpet. Be present to your feelings and then decide to talk to him when you are less attached to his reaction. As always, being in receptive mode will help you come to this place.

Sound advice. While writing this book, I see the perfection of the interaction with Datta, so you could show me how I need to work with being non-reactive with him. That brought up quite a bit of emotion for me. If I don't deal with this, it could take our relationship in a direction I don't want it to go.

He has his inner work to do, and he knows that. But if you can stay focused on bringing light to your own shadows and judgments more than being concerned with his, he will eventually relax that amount of challenge he presents. His resistance feeds off your resistance.

The ones closest to you can best show you how much inner work is still left to do.

Absolutely!

....

Contemplative Question:
How do you calm yourself down when an emotion surfaces that you want to express?

Access this chapter's guided practice in the *Unshakable Inner Peace* course at: UnshakableSeries.com

CHAPTER TWENTY-ONE: LOOKING IN

What other steps must I take to transition from a relatively happy human to a fully awakened being?

> The answer is within, literally. When you feel emotion, go inside the emotion. When you feel fear go inside the fear. When you want to feel Divine presence, go inside the subtle core of your body. When you want to see with your Universal eyes, look inward to the center of your head.

Do you mean to go within, but don't tell any mental story about my experience?

> Correct. Just focus inward with awareness and presence. Don't let your mind touch it with its conclusions or drama. The ego is on the constant lookout. The eyes of the separate self look outward to remain safe and to strategize how to get its needs met. The physical body has been trained to orient the eyes outward. You need to train your physical eyes to look mostly within. Orient your eyes, so you always have one eye looking in and one eye out.

I think I know what you mean. I do this when I'm coaching someone. One eye is on them to read what's happening with their physical, emotional, and energetic bodies, while the other eye peers inward to what I intuit. That one eye inward also allows me to keep a check on my ego or any resistance to what the client shares. When I don't get a clear signal from the client as to where to go next in the coaching session, I look inward to sense my spiritual guidance more clearly.

I've trained myself to have at least one eye inward when I'm on stage. I can look at and connect with the audience but focus at the same time on my internal landscape. That way, I can check if I feel grounded and connected to a song's emotion or the story or teaching point I share. I try to practice this in conversations with people too.

> Do you notice when you have both eyes out and lose your inward presence?

I've definitely lost this inward orientation during some of the State of the Union meetings with Datta. If I'm frustrated or emotionally flooded, my focus narrows toward him, and I become attached to him communicating with me in a certain way.

> The next time you notice both eyes focused outwards, look inward and intentionally track more of your internal landscape. As you do this in more interactions, you'll start to have your eyes look inward naturally. You'll create a new habit for your eyes from this practice.

Can I take a moment to shift back and forth between eyes out and eyes in?

Of course.

Looking outward engages my mind to name and judge what I see. When I look inward, I feel peace without judgment.

Looking inward relaxes you.

Occasionally, in my early twenties, someone would occasionally comment on how intense my eyes were. One acquaintance went to the trouble to point out how protruding my eyes were and how it felt like I was constantly staring her down. I didn't understand what she was talking about until around fifteen years later, when I saw a video of me performing at that age and it looked like I had bug eyes. They were staring at everyone, and that was what she was talking about. Nowadays, when I look in the mirror, I see they have relaxed back in my head more so.

> You've practiced looking inward for so long that it shows up physically. That's what happens. When you focus your energy, it affects the physical. The more you relax and receive, the more you appear relaxed and receptive. The more your heart opens, the more radiant you will look. The less you worry, the fewer lines you'll have between your eyebrows.

If I have fewer lumpy thoughts, will that help my thighs?

Cute.

In as many moments as possible, ask yourself, "What eyes am I looking out with, my ego eyes or my essential nature eyes?" That question alone can invite your focus back inward.

When the ego-eyes look outward to track the external environment, it makes you do things, say stuff, talk too much, or keep quiet—whatever helps meet their needs. You will not act unconsciously if you can switch eyes and look through your essential nature eyes.

I assume time in meditation would help me look within more. Do you have any advice for meditation?

Meditation is a broader topic than you might think. We'll get to the depth of that topic in due time. First, practice anything that will help relax the mind, sink into the internal space of your body, and anything that puts you in a receptive and non-resistant state.

What is your favorite way to meditate?

I rest my awareness in the center of my pelvis, which I call 'Home.' I then allow any mental or emotional tension without trying to change anything. I sense the length of the vertical core channel running through my body. I let the present moment take me somewhere versus trying to meditate to get somewhere.

That last point is something you missed in the early phases of your teaching meditation but is a valuable insight for you and your students now. Meditation isn't about getting somewhere. It's not about trying to get the mind to stay quiet so you can get a gold star for that meditation session. It's about dropping all tools and techniques that attempt to get you to an end goal or a specific state, since all results and states are temporary. When you focus on things that are temporary, you are not focused inward on what is constantly present. Instead, meditation is about becoming a receptive vessel, so the Infinite dimension of awareness can be perceived and experienced through your Earth Suit.

I had to reread that last sentence a few times to let it sink in. You pack a lot of wisdom into every sentence. How much should I meditate a day?

Your twice-daily routine of thirty minutes or more each time seems to agree with you.

I can sustain that, but I doubt most people would enjoy the prescription of one hour of meditation per day.

The length of time can differ between people, given their lifestyles and what stage of their spiritual journey they are at. Your ideal time is longer than ever because you enjoy the experience and have found your stride with meditation. Meditation is one of the best ways to unwind the residue of resistance that keeps enlightenment veiled from you. There will be a time in the future when you'll feel called to meditate for hours or days at a time. When you get that call, follow it. Meditation is a portal to the enlightenment experience.

Just as crucial as more extended meditation sits are the "mini meditations" when you walk, talk, and take action.

Is one 20-minute meditation daily enough for most to live in an enlightened space?

It's not about the numbers. Once you have realized what you really are and inner peace becomes your consistent experience, that length of time will be enough to live in that space, though you'll probably feel the desire for more.

It's a different story if you're not living in that space consistently. That short period would make the process of unwinding contractions difficult. For most people, it takes 20 or 30 minutes to unwind the mind and body enough to become receptive. It would be nice to hang out there for a while. True meditation requires receptivity. I think, personally, for you, you won't get to the openness and receptivity that allows for true meditation unless you are in a 30-minute session or longer.

I don't think I've ever correlated a sitting meditation with receptivity. I've felt the primary reason for sitting meditation is to relax the mind, witness my thoughts, feelings, and sensations, and let them pass through without grasping anything.

You describe a mindfulness practice. Conversely, meditation occurs when you slide into the dimension of Being, and abide in that space. For that to happen, you need to be very receptive.

So it's a subtle difference?

Subtle but significant.

Is there any other way I should 'go within'?

Write. You should write every day whenever you can. You have a wide receptive channel open, which we see in your speaking, but insight also wants to come through your writing. There are many other books that want to come through you. Writing will shift you into the receptive state, so lean into that.

This writing retreat has given me the experience of being receptive, and each day I feel more expanded. I don't think I've ever had multiple days in a row before where I can enjoy being on the receptive side of things. It sure doesn't hurt to be in Hawaii. The massage therapists at the resort have magical hands. Not as good as Datta's, but close. The morning walks on the beach put me in my feminine essence.

The longer you remain in a receptive state, the better. That's why certain kinds of retreats are so powerful for the awakening process. You might want to look for more retreats that specifically train you to be receptive for more extended periods. This writing retreat is doing this. Silent meditation retreats can do this. Vacations, where you unplug from all gadgets, can do this. I would also recommend getting more silence and alone time, in general, to practice being in your receptive body.

Are there other steps I can take to transition from a relatively happy human to a fully awakened being?

Yes. To not give a hoot about what anyone else thinks of you.

I would say that's easier said than done.

And I would say you're right, but that makes it no less important.

When you're in the public eye or a business leader, it throws you into a fishbowl where people can look in and pass judgment. Even though I'm showered with appreciation, the more people that follow me, the more people there will be who don't like something I do. It's simple math. Some don't keep their critique of me to themselves but post it on social media and write emails to my customer service team that outline why I'm out of integrity in some way, according to their worldview. I finally got it through my thick skull that what they think about me has more to do with them than with me. Why does someone believe that I speak superficially about topics, and another thinks the refinement and depth of my approach is refreshing?

It's the eyes they see with.

I'm getting better at not caring what others think of me, but one situation pierced my heart last year. A friend told me that one of my past clients told her I was doing business "in old patriarchal ways." I wasn't hurt by what my past client said; she had already built a reputation with me of being judgmental. The sting came when my friend decided to believe this client and presume I was running our business that way. It brought up my core issues of being abandoned and misunderstood by a friend and not looking good in her eyes. I never spoke to her about how unfairly judged I felt. I tried to let it go, but the tension stayed in the background of our relationship, and the result was that I didn't see her much anymore. I recently admitted that I pulled away from our relationship as my image was tarnished. My reaction was just as much about me as it was about her. When I had that insight, the built-up tension vanished. I was able to take responsibility for the way I reacted and didn't put it all on her.

Very good.

Datta and I have discussed how we want to come to all our relationships being 100% responsible for how we feel. That has helped us so much to not blame each other for our feelings but to acknowledge them and ask for support. I also finally have a practice to use when I start to care too much about what others think of me. I remind myself, "What they think of me is none of my business." People are going to think what they think, largely due to their own beliefs and past experience. I can't control that.

No, you can't.

Are there other steps I need to take for this transition from a relatively happy human to a fully awakened being?

> Of course, but don't put weight on the word "fully" in your question. Think about the consistency of being in the receptive state and looking at the world with your Universal eyes, which are aware of the self-aware observer. It's about consistency now. You have many moments when you are in this experience of being an awakened being.

Many moments? I don't think so.

> These are the moments when your eyes water because the love pouring through you is immense. When you feel as expansive as the entire universe, and it emanates through you and off your body in all directions. When everyone else is triggered by someone or something, and you are not. When your mind is still, and there's no tension in your body. When you know something about someone that you couldn't know with human powers alone. These experiences will become more consistent, and being more receptive will help.

I feel lighter as you talk about it. I look forward to more of the blissful moments that I already feel.

> When the ego takes the background, it allows Infinite love, power, and knowing to take the foreground. You see less with your ego eyes and more with your essence eyes.

Specific experiences serve as catalysts for more Divine seeing. On this awakening path, you will know you are Divine. You will get lighter and more radiant.

There are such things as blissful enlightenment moments. But there will be an awakening in you beyond these moments. That is coming. Enlightenment is not just about having experiences of receptivity and non-resistance. An awakening can happen through your mind, where you'll see your essential nature in a particular way. It's difficult to explain, but I'll be here to help you understand it as you go through it. For now, don't focus on tremendous blissful experiences. Instead, ask in as many moments as possible, "What eyes am I seeing with?"

Are you reminding me to take one step at a time and not get too far ahead of myself?

Yes. The spiritual awakening experience is like peeling back an onion. You have to peel the outer layers before getting to the inner ones. If you chop the onion in half to get to the inner layers quicker, you'll still have the outer layers stuck to you. You may glimpse the inner dimension, but the outer one won't be released.

Am I in the middle of the onion, peeling its mid-layer?

You may well be peeling that mid layer, but all that's important is peeling the layer you are on.
Does that make sense?

Contemplative Question:
What do I experience when I turn both eyes inward

Access this chapter's guided practice in the *Unshakable Inner Peace* course at: UnshakableSeries.com

CHAPTER TWENTY-TWO: ENERGETIC MUSCLES

As you have said, "Where your attention goes, energy flows." When I turn my attention inward with a receptive body, I can only assume my ego will become quieter.

You can bet on it.

I see so many people not present in their bodies. Even so-called "Deeply spiritual" people are in their mental meanderings most of the time! They don't have the bodily awareness to be present in the energetic internal space of their body. They don't have intimate experiences with their energy field.

Perhaps not, but that's where you come in. You saw this relevant issue with people on a spiritual path. You gave them an easy-to-understand map to embodiment and present within their physical and energetic bodies.

Once your clients get the fundamentals, you help them create greater connection between their physical and energetic bodies. This part of the puzzle is essential on the path to enlightenment. If your energy is all over the place and not properly anchored in the physical body, keeping your mind from chattering and having emotional reactions that cause suffering is hard.

All the energetic and embodiment practices and meditations you teach in your *Art of Feminine Presence* and *Art of Masculine Presence* trainings help with this unification of energy and the physical body.

Are there practices you can suggest that help create a more substantial alignment between the physical and energetic bodies?

Being embodied in your Vertical Core and containing your energy field within an energetic, solid boundary helps. It keeps you focused inwardly. Moving your physical and energetic bodies at the same time with a 50/50 balance is perfect. To do this, you must be aware of your energy as much as your physicality.

I tend to be more physical in my movements than energetic. I constantly have to remind myself to walk with a lighter foot and feel my energetic hips swaying.

The Presence Meditation you teach focuses on embodiment, receptivity, and opening energy centers. There are other practices, but that's a strong start. Your readers can investigate your *Art of Feminine Presence* and *Art of Masculine Presence* trainings for more instructions on practices that work exceptionally well.

Why is it so important for enlightenment to be embodied in our physical and energetic forms?

Because you experience enlightenment through the body-mind instrument, your essential nature is Infinite boundless awareness. There is no start or end to what you are. Therefore, your essential nature doesn't need to become enlightened or experience anything different. When you ask, "Can I reach enlightenment this lifetime?" What you really what to know is, "Can I have the experience of knowing my true essence through my mind and body?"

You're right. I don't want to just intellectually know my essence from a book from the spirituality shelf in Barnes and Noble. I want to experience the peace and happiness that comes with this realization.

And you want it to stick!

Absolutely! I want to feel expansion and non-resistance to whatever shows up.

Embodiment is crucial as it allows the experience of your eternal essential nature through your energy centers. It's also vital if you want to abide in that place. If you jump out of your body and into your head bubble, you will be using your ego eyes. If you jump out of your heart, you won't know if it's open, which is problematic because being open to receive is what offers the experience of enlightenment through your heart. It's important to be able to manage the internal realms of your body if you want to allow more flow of Infinite presence through your experience. You start the embodiment journey by sensing yourself from inside your body.

What helps me to stay in my body is to focus my awareness down into my belly center. I use that space as an anchor to sense myself from inside my body. This means dropping my awareness, step by step, down the vertical core of my body until I feel I am at least 3 inches below the navel and back toward the spine. I locate the center of my pelvic bowl with my attention. Then energy flows there.

Once anchored in my pelvis, I direct attention to other energy centers along my vertical core and anchor myself there. I think I've become good at splitting my attention evenly to all energy centers.

> Indeed, you have. This invites a more expanded dimension of sensing yourself.

A quirky analogy I like to use is a spacecraft docking at a space station. When I dock my energy body into my physical body, I feel fantastic.

> That's a great example.

To do that, I start to become aware of my vertical core. I imagine the energy centers along my vertical core channel are docking points, and my physical centers are docking points too. For example, I'll sense the center of my physical chest connecting with the energy center of my chest. Then, I'll do the same with the center of my head, my belly center, and finally, the other centers. With that focus, I sense a gathering of energy into the internal space of my physical body. Once I feel locked into the core of my body, I focus on the vertical energetic channel that goes upwards into the heavens and downwards into the earth. All this creates a feeling like something else is looking through my eyes rather than my small self. I feel the warmth of my heart. I feel grounded. My mind is quiet.

> That's a great practice to have the mind, body, and spirit become more coherent. Coherence breeds balance and openness. It's hard to be attached and resistant to the moment you are in this kind of energetic alignment.
> You've built great energetic muscles so far. They will serve you well as you move into unchartered territory in the not-too-distant future.

Can you tell me more about energetic muscles?

> They represent the ability to contain and not leak your energy, to raise the frequency of that energy, to direct your energy towards what you want, and to receive universal energy through the body. You already teach this with precision and see things clearly in energetic form. I know you have questions, but first, let me ask you what you think are the essential energetic muscles to build that lead to spiritual awakening.

I would say energetic muscles refer to the ability to contain more energy in each energy center, and being more embodied in the vertical core channel. Then, not constricting in any energy center. Open energy centers create less constriction in one's thoughts, feelings, and life force. Perhaps most importantly, it would mean feeling spacious and transparent in my energy field, so my mind won't be so controlling and resistant.

How was that?

All good answers. I would add one more to the list, though.
Drum roll please . . .
The energetic muscle of RECEIVING.

Oh, right. I forgot that one.

Yeah, you did. The fundamental practice you kept forgetting
in your training, Receptive Body, is a great way to build this
muscle.
Take a moment and become aware of the sun. It's a perfect
temperature day to be in the sun.

It is perfect, even for my fair skin. I love drinking in the sun's rays
while walking around the resort. When I take a break on one of the
benches overlooking the water, I turn my palms up and imagine
the sun rays entering my veins and blessing me with more Vitamin
D.

Imagine your arms receiving the perfect temperature sun
rays right at this moment.

I feel my body relax, and a smile comes to my face.

Imagine stretching back on a lounge chair, receiving the
perfect temperature sun rays through your whole body.

My smile widens, and my heart opens. Nothing has to change.
Everything is perfect.

This is what happens when you become more receptive. The body lets go, so the energy centers can let go and open, and the mind follows, seeing that everything is perfect.

Being receptive to the sun is easy, but it's a bit harder with annoying humans.

That's why I want you to build the energetic muscle of receiving, so it's impossible to offer resistance to any person, no matter how irritating they are. You can stay in an open, receptive place, without taking on all their refuse. When you stay in your own experience and don't shut down your receptivity, it breeds openness and non-resistance.

This means I can stay happy no matter how obnoxious the drunk guy is at the bar, thinking he's God's gift, singing at the top of his lungs, "*I've Got Friends in Low Places*"? All he did last night was drown out the guy on stage who sounded great.

Did you react to Mr. Out-of-Tune-Karaoke-King?

Not really. I felt sorry for the Hawaiian local on stage, but then I caught myself in the assumption that he wouldn't enjoy this guy singing along with him. I questioned the assumption as you told me to do earlier in our conversation and just let it go. That brought me back to my happy place, and I could focus on receiving the beautiful people at my table.

What did you do energetically to receive your friends last night?

I can't say I did anything on purpose. When I think back, I felt open and relaxed and didn't need to change anything.

> You were in the same energetic space as you were when you contemplated receiving the sun. You can use that "receiving the sun" analogy to help you be more receptive to others. Focus on being in your receptive body when people speak to you. Feel your energy centers becoming less constricted when you share time with someone and notice the intimacy that soars.

I have shared from the stage many times that people might resist the practices I teach because they create more intimacy with others than they're used to. People can become embarrassed by intimacy and don't know how to act when they are so open. People guard against being in their bodies because it creates intimacy. I see it in the checkout line at the grocery store. I see it when someone meets a new person at a party. I had to get used to feeling more intimate with people—which took a while.

Do you have any other explanations or instructions regarding building energetic muscles?

> You stated earlier that one energetic muscle worth building is the ability to contain more energy in each energy center, which leads to being more embodied in your vertical core. You're on target. Another definition for the containment of energy is to build and keep reserves. When anyone's resources are depleted, they tend to be more in their ego.

I can relate. Don't come near this Taurus girl when she's hungry or tired. You'll see an ego gone wild.

> It's the same when someone hasn't received much sustenance energetically.

Really?

> Absolutely. They are also in lack. When someone lacks energy, they naturally try to get it from somewhere—from other people, substances, partying, gossiping, etc. When someone is full of energy, they don't look to external circumstances as much to make them fulfilled.
>
> There is an abundance of energy to receive. You can receive it from the earth, you can receive it from higher dimensional realms, and you can receive it by receiving and allowing the love from other people to land with you. The essential practice that takes you to the gateway of unshakable inner peace is receiving so much incredible energy that it's almost impossible for you to close down to receiving. It's like lifting weights. Your strength builds over time, so remind people to be patient. For over a decade, you've been diligently building energetic muscles through various mind-body practices. Now you are ready for a significant shift in consciousness.

I believe the Vertical Core and Light Globe practices I teach are most important to strengthening the energetic muscles we just explored.

I agree. Take a moment now to feel your Vertical Core.

Hmm. I'm experiencing brighter energy, a quieter mind, and a sense of safety.

Yes.

I know my vertical core is halfway from the front of my body to the back, but when I'm embodied in that core it feels like I'm leaning back further in my body than halfway.

That's only because you are so used to being oriented forward. Your mind is always chasing the next thing, which makes you energetically lean forward rather than lean back into the moment.

When I'm in my vertical core, I feel no impulse to chase anything. I see how the vertical core keeps me present.

Now, take a moment to feel your bio-energetic field, which you call the Light Globe.

This is pleasurable.

What exactly are you experiencing?

I feel larger, lighter, and happier. All my mind chatter has disappeared. It always feels wonderful when I experience the energy glow that emanates through and around me.

You are experiencing your own glow. When that happens, you slide into another dimension of awareness. It shows you that you are not just your body and mind, but also the energetic field that pervades them. This should not be mistaken for the dimension of Infinite awareness, but it's a bridge to that.

When I feel my Light Globe, I know I am more extensive than what I see in the mirror.

There are not enough mirrors to show you how immense you are.

Thanks. Well, that is an excellent place to pause. It's nearing the end of the day, and I've enjoyed this enlightening experience with you. I appreciate you walking me through my fear and anger after Datta's response to my book. I don't feel any residue from that uncomfortable interaction with him anymore. Thank you for reminding me how everything we are talking about comes back to the importance of receiving.

I'm physically tired but energetically high. What should I do tonight to support myself to be fresh in the morning?

Take a walk. Exercise in a way that feels good. Then have a bath, and don't overthink the book. Let it go. I'll be here to help pull it together tomorrow.

Who are you, anyway?

I will tell you soon. You are stubborn sometimes, and fortunate that I am not easily irritated.

I'm a triple Taurus. I would call my nature determined.

Of course you would. Yet you are stubborn and determined. Neither is better than the other. Every part of you serves a purpose, and there is a purpose in every energy you have access to as a human being.

Are you pointing to the Shadow Work I teach?

Yes.

....

Contemplative Question:
What do I experience when embodied in my Vertical Core?

Access this chapter's guided practice in the *Unshakable Inner Peace* course at: UnshakableSeries.com

CHAPTER TWENTY-THREE: THE DARK SIDE

Shadow Work is something that came across my path early on. A friend gave me Debbie Ford's book, *Dark Side of the Light Chasers*. I was drawn to the term *Light Chasers*. That's what I felt I was. I wanted to understand who I was and why I operated the way I did. I felt I was an old soul in a young, naive body.

Ford based her work on Carl Jung's research for the spiritual seeker. Jung and her both argued that it's essential to not just move your attention toward positive, lovable qualities but also to look at the dark and seemingly unlovable qualities. This profound psychological practice of Shadow Work helps people manage the impulses they often either ignore or unconditionally surrender to. When a part of oneself is discounted, we either don't use it when it could be helpful, or it comes up with a forceful blast because it's been suppressed for so long.

Before I moved to America in 2002, I was part of a small group of committed Light Chasers who lived in and around Melbourne. We decided to gather for a day to explore the information in the book. By lunchtime, there was no shortage of shadows on my list that I considered unlovable.

What was on your list of shadow qualities, Rachael Jayne?

It was a pretty big list. I would have been mortified if anyone had considered me any one of these:

- Needy
- Arrogant
- Superficial
- Bitchy
- Ditsy
- Angry
- Stupid
- Unoriginal

Should I go on? There were more that filled my journal that day.

That's a significant list of shadows.

I couldn't imagine why a spiritual person should embrace any of these things. I thought becoming more spiritual was about getting rid of these listed qualities, especially ones like being a bitch or thinking I was better than anyone else.

And what's your understanding of the Shadow self now?

Now I try to see that there are parts of our psyche we are conscious of and parts we are not. Just because we are unaware of certain parts or suppress them doesn't mean they don't show up in our behavior and affect our lives. They certainly do, and are acted out from the "shadow" of our unconscious. This acting out is not helpful most of the time because when we are unaware of a part of ourselves, we don't have control over how to use or not use it. It happens automatically.

For example, if someone isn't aware that they are judgmental and fights against the possibility of being judgmental, then being judgmental remains in their unconscious. When something happens that triggers them to be judgmental, they still pass judgement, but don't realize they are doing so.

On the other hand, if someone acknowledges they are judgmental, it's easier to understand there might be times that are appropriate to judge and times not to.

> Examples, please. When do you think would be a time that would be appropriate to judge, and when would it not be?

If I'm trying to figure out whether to hire or fire someone from our team, I would say it's not only appropriate, but important and necessary to judge. I need to use all my skills to determine whether they could do an excellent job and make a judgment call. On the other hand, on a personal level, I would not find it helpful to be morally judgmental about someone's choices if I didn't know the person or the whole story.

Another good example would be a first date. If somebody is looking for a long-term relationship, and they're on a first date with someone, they would need to judge whether the other person is a potential fit for that long-term relationship, and then decide whether they would go on a second date. Fast-forward a few years, and say they are in intimate partnership, then that judgment can be turned way down. However, it's not turned off, because in extreme situations (and sometimes not extreme situations for less committed people) the decision might be made to leave a relationship.

Well said.

During that gathering in Melbourne, I grasped the concept of Shadow. It is the process of uncovering parts of yourself that have been repressed or hidden and integrating them into your conscious mind and behaviors. But I didn't understand the importance of committing to my ongoing Shadow Work until I moved to America a year later when I found myself on the receiving end of behaviors that came from the shadows of those whom I had considered some of the most spiritual people.

It was a shock, wasn't it?

Oh yes! I had naively thought someone on a spiritual path would be a lovely person by default. I thought being on such a path would heal one of all passive-aggressiveness, envy, abusive tendencies, and arrogance. At least they wouldn't yell at their friends, I figured.

Just because someone is spiritually oriented doesn't mean they're doing their psychological work. Spiritual and psychological work tend to land in two distinctly separate categories. Giving repressed memories and personality tendencies attention is very different from spending more time on the meditation cushion focused on the Infinite space of awareness. You practice them separately, though they support each other.

How do they do that?

Becoming more aware of your psychological patterns can help your spiritual growth because you start to see these patterns as temporary and ever-changing and they are not what is fundamental to you. On the other hand, time in the spiritual practice of meditation can help you see that these patterns originate from a void, and there is no point in beating yourself up for the negative thoughts you have. This starts to slow the mind's compulsions down.

I've seen the sweetest of ladies get jealous and gossip. I saw spiritual gurus react to petty things and shame others in public. I saw so-called trustworthy leaders in the community cheat on their partners. I saw facilitators sleeping with their students. The behavior was so opposite to the images that I've never forgotten the importance of being humble enough to do my own Shadow Work. As I continue to choose a "Shadow of the Month" to work on for myself and my clients, the list of people that trigger me shrinks in size every month or so. I love teaching this work because I believe it frees people.

Shadow Work is essential to what you teach in the psychological realm. The ego has such a strong grip on people's experience that it compels them to do things that are not who they really want to be. When you bring more Shadows to the light, you become more receptive, so in turn, less resistant and less run by your psychological patterns.

I love that.

Shadow Work helps you offer no resistance to any part of the psyche. When there is no resistance to a quality that needs to be expressed, you can move on to the next moment without judgment of yourself or another. When you bring a shadow part to light, you can see both the destructive and helpful versions. You'll be able to witness these parts and make more of a conscious choice about when and how to use them rather than have them control your life. You won't resist; you'll choose.

Shadow Work is another practice for non-resistance.

Yes.

Even though looking at the parts of myself I don't want to see feels awful and embarrassing, I need to do so to not be resistant to anything or anyone. Resistance usually doesn't end up pretty.

Do you remember any time this past week when you behaved in a way you didn't want to?

I do. I was coaching someone on Zoom who kept repeating the same pattern, which was getting more annoying by the second. They kept droning on with the same excuses I'd heard for months. I wanted to shake them to break them out of it. I was curter than I wanted to be, and I'm sure they felt my frustration.

A curt reaction could be destructive, or it could be helpful, depending on the situation.

I guess so. I know from being a coach for over twenty years that a curt reaction can help break a pattern.

Exactly.

It can be helpful to shock them and interrupt the usual psychological process to make it easier to create a new way. However, in this case, I would love to say that I consciously attempted to break their pattern, but I wasn't conscious of that. I was just irritated and couldn't hold it in anymore.

What was the quality in them that made you irritated?

It was their wishy-washy, whiney, no backbone, no "just do it" attitude.

This year, any of these would be good 'Shadows of the Month' for you.

Yuck! I don't want to be wishy-washy. I don't want to be weak. I don't want to be a coward.

Your reaction tells us both they are all Shadows of yours.

I know. I get it, but I don't like it.

There is a time, place, and reason for just about everything. Sometimes it's helpful to use the energy of wishy-washy, weak, or cowardly. Don't resist these parts of you. They are a part of every human. Become aware of them so you can use them to serve—not hurt, which the opposite can do. How might being wishy-washy, weak or a coward benefit you?

I need to think about this for a minute.

Take your time.

I guess being wishy-washy could benefit me when I don't need to make a fast decision that could get me in hot water. I can see that owning my weakness can allow someone better than me—or in a better position than me—to help me. I can see that being a coward might protect me from harm in the right circumstance.

Aren't there times when it's appropriate to be needy?

I suppose when you need support from another.

Aren't there times when it's helpful to be angry?

Absolutely. When someone continues not to respect my boundaries, or I need to defend against a perpetrator.

Are there times when it's best to be a perpetrator?

That's a hard one. Maybe not.

Is there any time that causing harm to another is valid and in integrity with you?

If I saw someone hurting an innocent person and I had a chance to stop it by hurting the villain, I would do that.

> Are there times that it might be appropriate for you to be the villain and for someone else to be the victim?

I can think of an actual example when I played the villain. Sort of. I let go of one of our longest and most loyal employees. With her, the company couldn't reach the next level. It was a tough decision, and I greatly loved this person. I knew it could put her in harm's way, as it would be hard for her to get another job. We gave her a severance package, but I'm sure she felt like I was the perpetrator and she the victim. I can't blame her for thinking that. I did cause harm to her feelings, to her happiness, and to her financial security—at least for a while—but in my heart, it was the right thing to do for the whole team. Once we let her go, she cut all communication with us. I had hoped a few friendly emails would keep the relationship intact, but it didn't.

> That must have been hard for you and Datta.

It was. Earlier, you said Shadow Work helps us to be more receptive in many ways. What are the other ways?

> Shadow Work can stop you from bypassing parts of the personality that cause problems in your relationships. Whatever you avoid sticks to you. You create your own private version of the movie Groundhog Day, wondering why you keep creating the same relationship issues. A

resistant stance to a part of your psyche creates resistance in your mind, heart, gut, and energy field. What is the opposite of resistance?

Receptivity?

Very good. When you are open in your mind, heart, and gut and feel more transparent through your respective energetic field, you are more receptive without even trying to be.

That's been my experience with integrating the toughest shadow of my life, which has been arrogance. I didn't want anyone to think I was arrogant or thought I was better than them. That's why I was having a hard time earlier worrying if my readers would think I was arrogant. But integrating this Shadow has given me more freedom to express myself and not worry as much about what others think of me.

The more you bring parts of yourself out of the unconscious and into the conscious you free up more life force because your energy centers are more open. Your energy centers are not trying to push this Shadow self down.

I use this analogy. Imagine you take something you don't want to express and push it behind you. You keep it at bay with all your might because you don't want anyone else to see that you have this part within you. Notice how much energy it takes to keep this part of you at bay! Because there is so much intensity, it's impossible for your attention not to go there. When you have the courage to let go and integrate that part, you don't have your life force going toward your fist. You receive a release of energy through your core and, in turn, feel more joy and vitality, which helps with being non-resistant.

> It ends up with you being in a more receptive body.

Are there other ways Shadow Work makes one more receptive?

> When you do your Shadow Work, you are not defending your ego. You are more receptive because you are more compassionate. You can see in another how hard it is not to act out in unhealthy ways since you've seen it in yourself. This work is a bold move towards radical compassion towards yourself. Only when you have true compassion for yourself can you have compassion for others.

I've been working with the shadow of "defensive" recently. I chose it because my husband tells me at least once every two weeks when I am being defensive. Sometimes I'm aware I am. Other times I feel very calm and believe he is misreading the situation. At times it has felt like calling me defensive is his way of being defensive. Either way, I have huge resistance to the word "defensive."

> Does Datta tell you to stop being defensive?

No. Usually, he'll ask me if I'm feeling defensive, though sometimes he says he feels I'm defensive. He does that less than he used to, however.

> How have you been working with your defensiveness?

When he asks if I feel defensive, I look closer by going inside my body to see whether I'm feeling defensive. I feel into my nervous system to see if it feels protective, and it often does. I feel into my level of openness to Datta, which is typically on a spectrum. If I replay a moment that happened earlier in the day, I slow things down so I can pinpoint when I first started feeling defensive. If I catch my defensiveness in the moment, I breathe into my vertical core, particularly my womb space.

> That sounds like a good practice.

As I gain more awareness of when I'm defensive, I feel more receptive to him. I'm not as triggered when he gets irritated at me and considers me defensive. Sometimes I can rest in my womb space and let him have those judgments without trying to get him to see his defensive patterns. Sometimes I can't. I'm a work in progress.

> Perfectly said. That's human life.

Do you have any tips on best integrating and loving my shadows?

> In your retreats, you start people exploring gracefully with
> two primary questions: "How are you this shadow part?"
> or "How have you been this shadow part in the past?"

I feel this question allows people to pry open a closed mind and be curious about how this part is in them and how it's operated.

> The second question you ask is, "What is the virtue or
> positive quality of this shadow part?" This question points

towards finding out what could be helpful about this part, as we just explored with you. It can be a difficult question to answer.

Embracing and integrating Shadows opens the door for the magic to happen. Those with the courage to do this will have all aspects of humanity at their disposal. The range of expression of this person will be unlimited. They can choose *how* to act and not be run by old psychological patterns that no longer serve. I am happy that Shadow work is a big focus in your programs and retreats. It's often a missing link in the awakening journey.

If I feel my nervous system getting triggered, does this mean I have a shadow around that person or situation?

Not necessarily. It could just be a trigger from a past experience, and basic psychological conditioning is at play. For example, say someone yelled at you and grabbed you from behind and ended up hurting you years ago. If someone snuck up behind you today and yelled something at you—even if they didn't touch you—your nervous system would probably have a reaction. But it doesn't mean that's a shadow making itself known.

Can we shift a shadow just by being in the vertical core of our body?

No. That wouldn't be enough on its own to integrate that shadow. However, it will help you not react and have more compassion for that shadow. To integrate it fully, there must be a psychological "seeing" of the shadow and making friends with it.

Got it. Are there shadows of organizations? I feel as though I have experienced them in the past.

You certainly have. The leader or leaders create the dominant energy of an organization. Their inability to see what they are resisting and judging affects everyone in different ways.

I look at my watch and am surprised to see that we only have an hour to go until our time to write together in this retreat is up. I suddenly feel tense, and have the sense that I'm running out of time, which doesn't feel good. I don't know if we'll have time to finish our conversation.

We should talk about time, Rachael Jayne. Your relationship with time creates a significant roadblock between where you are now and living an enlightened life.

Contemplative Question:
What are your Shadow parts?

Access this chapter's guided practice in the *Unshakable Inner Peace* course at: UnshakableSeries.com

CHAPTER TWENTY-FOUR: OUT OF TIME

Is the pace we are moving at a problem?

> If your pace is too fast, it can hinder the process of receptivity and awakening. However, it's not a problem in the grander scheme of things. Something will occur sooner or later to slow you down if you go too fast. It's why injuries happen a lot of the time. It's why dark nights of the soul happen. These create a time to reflect on your path and how you've veered from your soul's mission. Sometimes a significant life challenge is the only way to slow someone down. Would you prefer to slow down on your own or from something to cause you to slow down?

I'll take option A, thank you very much, and slow down on my own. A severe back injury seventeen years ago put me out of action for years with chronic pain. It was my dark night of the soul. Looking back now, I see it was a way to set me on a new path. My back is now a lot stronger, but it can still be a way to slow me down when needed.

Last year, three days before the most significant event of my year, I woke up and couldn't get out of bed. Ice did nothing. Datta's miracle massage hands didn't help the way they usually did. Ibuprofen didn't even touch the pain. I was forced to rest and surrender all I wanted to get done before the event. The next morning, I woke up in even more pain and couldn't walk alone. I had images of being wheeled onto the stage in a wheelchair in front of three hundred people. I couldn't imagine how this predicament would turn in my favor. I'd never had a steroid shot in my life, but it seemed like the only option at the moment like this. I was desperate. I couldn't refund all three hundred tickets. Most attendees had already boarded a plane for Colorado when I was butt up in the air, waiting for the needle.

As I lay under the covers, watching my assistant pack my suitcase, I was struck by how this injury had given me exactly what I needed but felt I couldn't ask for—a few days to be with myself and my intentions for the event. I surrendered to the time I wanted, and by the miracle of modern medicine, I was back in heels as the event kicked off.

> The body is one of your best allies to help you restore balance.

I'm learning that lesson, although I wish I were a quicker study.

> There we go with another worry about speed. Ponder this: Are you going at the right pace for your spiritual awakening or too fast?

Most days, I'm probably going too fast. I get irritated when my time is wasted, or I can't fit in as much as I want. My answer is usually to think and work faster.

> And your relationship with time is one of your biggest hindrances to enlightenment.

Yikes. Tell me more.

> You're good at being present when you meditate, coach someone, or feel there is plenty of time. But your to-do list is long and always will be because you're an open channel for creativity. You'll always have more books, courses, and entrepreneurial ideas than you can humanly keep up with. The aim is not to cross everything off. Your human self will never keep up with your Source. You believe it's a problem when you don't keep up with your to-do list. This is not a problem.

It sure feels like a problem when I have deadlines to meet.

> Pause, and breathe this in. Never try to keep up with your to-do list. When you align with your higher guidance, which is a million times more expansive than your human self, you will have a long, fulfilling to-do list.

But my to-do list overwhelms me some days.

> Only because you fall into the illusion of linear time. There is only one unified experience of now, and everything happens within it. You don't experience this when you are overwhelmed because you experience time differently from the various dimensions of awareness we've discussed earlier. If you feel like you are running out of time, you are in the dimension of your body and mind. When you feel like there is unlimited time, you are in the dimension of your

essential self. If you think there is a past and a future, you are in the dimension of your body and mind. If you sense that this now experience is the same now experience you were in a few days ago when you took a moment to pause, you are in the dimension of your essential self. How you feel in relationship to time indicates how far away you are from the experience of your infinite self.

I've never had an experience where I sensed this moment of now was the same moment of now from any time in my past. I don't feel this moment now is the same as when I was twenty-something, first learning to meditate.

That's only because no one has brought it to your attention that this is the same now experience.

I notice you say "now experience" instead of "moment of now."

That's because when I say the word "moment," it makes you think in linear time: "This moment is this moment, and that moment was that moment." When you perceive from the dimension of your essential self, it is a felt experience of being within one continuous present moment.

I think I get that. Yes, I've had that experience.

Go to that place now.

Right now?

Yes. Be in the experience of now. Be nowhere else but right here, right now.

Okay, let me take a moment.

Sure, take a moment inside the now.

When I'm in this space, my mind is quiet. I see something circular. Are you putting a circle shape in my awareness?

Yes.

I see that the circle contains everything. In the center of the circle is a portal of some sort.

It's a portal to your Source. Everything is birthed and is contained in Source. Some call this Source God, Divine, Allah, Jehova, Krishna, or simply Universe. And that list goes on. Everything is contained in the one and only experience of now. That means you can change the reality of your future by focusing now, with thought and emotion, on what you want to experience. You can change the reality of your past as well.

That seems . . . impossible. How do I do that?

When you are in the now experience, how do you feel?

Peaceful, present, expansive, and warm.

When you look back at the years you were disabled with your back injury, how do you experience that now?

I experience it with deep gratitude and without pain. I'm grateful that Datta was with me to look after me, support me, and encourage me. I'm grateful for all the lessons that experience gave me.

What else do you notice when you are in the now experience?

I notice a gentle pressure at the back base of my head. My eyes are turned inward without me doing that on purpose. My energetic field feels contained and I'm in my vertical core, which feels like it holds me in the circular experience of now.

The energetic system changes when you are in this dimension of the Infinite now experience. You can stabilize the experience of now in two ways so it feels more like your natural state. These ways are two sides of the same coin. One way is to build the energetic and receptive muscles that pull you into the now experience without your mental effort. The other way is to go to an experience of now with your mental focus and relax the body into a receptive state. The energetics will start to shift on their own, which makes it easier and more automatic to return to this presence in the now experience.

Is this now experience the same now experience you were inside of when you first learned to meditate twenty years ago?

I believe it is. I can't tell you how I know that, but it's the same quality of experience. Everything becomes still.

> Is this now experience the same now experience as when you were meditating yesterday?

Yes. It's like I'm returning to something that will always be there.

> Well said. Would you like to move out of the now experience into the linear time dimension to see what happens?

Sure. I doubt I'll like it as much.

> Think about the body and how it needs to move through time and space to make your to-do list happen over the next few months.

When I think of linear time, I see a horizontal line going from past to future, and everything happens somewhere along this continuum. Energetically, I feel the gentle pressure at the top-back corner of my head, rather than further down when I was in the now experience. I bet if I watched a brain scan of myself, a different part of my brain would light up. My eyes feel more forward. We conversed earlier about the eyes looking inward or outward and how that affects the dimension of seeing. When I am attuned to linear time, my eyes look outward. I feel more stressed in this place, and less receptive.

I can perceive the two different dimensions of time. Thank you for guiding me into linear time, so I can compare it to the single now experience. I can now guess why my relationship with time is so important for enlightenment.

I'd love to hear more of your thoughts on that.

If I keep falling for the idea that time is linear, my body and mind will be pulled toward that linear experience and plan my life from a sense of limited time. That puts me directly into a reality where I must strive, protect, worry, etc. If I know I can move in and out of the same "now" experience, I get pulled toward the now experience. I don't sense my ego-personality when I'm in the now experience; I feel timelessness and spaciousness. Am I missing anything?

Great understanding. Your experience of linear time or timelessness affects how you relate to the ideas of death, attachment, protecting the image of your persona, and other fears that you need to unwind to move along the spiritual path.

So, how can it be true that there is an Infinite amount of time?

Because this now experience will never disappear. The vortex into this grand spaciousness isn't going to die. No matter what age I am or what body I am in, I can return to this place where there is more and more time.

Well done. And what's one thing you can do or be when you want to contact this Infinite time?

Be receptive?

> You've got it! Are you aware that you close off being receptive when you move too fast through life?

Sometimes. I mean, I always close off being receptive when I'm in speedy mode. When I rush, I can be more of a grumpy bum than anyone. Just ask Datta.

> I don't have to. I believe you. Here are the practical actions to take if you want to loosen your limited sense of time, which makes you rush. Give yourself more time in the morning. How you start your day predicts how you'll react to the day. Plan what you are going to do a little further in advance. You get caught running out of linear time, so you squish things into the spaces on your calendar where you could take a breather. This habit of yours hurts your work team as well. They're trying to move as fast as you and don't have enough downtime between tasks. When you are in the car, practice receptivity and slide into the now experience, even though it appears like you are going from point A to point B. You'll find it impossible to get angry at another driver when they're running late for an important meeting—or just running out of time.
>
> When you open your inbox, what is your dominant thought?

I always wish I didn't have to do this. I want to get past my email to focus on something I want to do.

Take the email block of time and ask yourself, how can I be in the now experience while I reply to email? In ancient times the saying was "Chop wood and carry water." The modern version is "Respond to emails and pack the dishwasher." Can you respond to your email or load the dishwasher with full presence?

That's a stretch.

Isn't stretching what you signed up for with this life?

It is.

Then don't be surprised when you get what you ask for. That full presence focus when you're doing tedious tasks that you don't love will be great practice because you get resentful when you're not doing extraordinary creative things but instead stuck with mundane tasks.

You are saying that the Divine is present in the mundane as well. Is that correct?

Precisely. It's your practice to find the Divine there and enjoy it.

I will take that challenge on. I'm awed by the amount of pleasure I feel through my body when I am in the experience of now.

It feels good because you are in non-resistance. If you lived in non-resistance, you'd feel this wonderful most of the time. It's why enlightenment is often described with words like bliss and euphoria. Enlightenment doesn't mean you'll be joyful all the time, but when the realization of what you are seeps into your cells, you'll mostly be somewhere between quiet peace and joyful ecstasy.

Joyful ecstasy is a good way to describe what I feel right now. You keep ushering me into more expansive feelings. Are you ready to tell me who you are?

Yes. This may be the most significant insight of all. Are you ready?

I am.

....

Contemplative Question:
What do you notice in the now experience?

Access this chapter's guided practice in the *Unshakable Inner Peace* course at: UnshakableSeries.com

CHAPTER TWENTY-FIVE: THE REVEAL

This voice you have been listening to and dictating is You.

How is that possible? Why does your voice sound so different from mine? Your perspective is also different, and there is a clear difference between when you speak and when I speak.

Notice the capital Y. I am the big You, not the small human you. The big You has an Infinite vantage point. Everyone has a big You. It doesn't perceive through the ego mind, like the human you does. The big You experiences everything from the realm of unconditional acceptance and knows it can never be damaged or corrupted. It knows its never-ending nature. The big You is perfectly interwoven into the field of Infinite awareness and possibilities. You have tapped into the same dimension Einstein was in when he received his visions. He received his insights through visuals, and you receive yours primarily through the auditory route.

Are you saying I wasn't channeling anything or anyone specifically?

If you want to use the term channel, you could say you were channeling a higher dimension of yourself.

Oh.

You sound disappointed. That might be a bit of ego coloring your vision.

I'm mainly just surprised. When people channel, I imagine them receiving information from a particular spiritual being or group of beings.

Humans can channel one of their angels, guides, or a group of spiritual guides. You have communed with the higher dimension of Your self, who has given you insight from the realm of infinite love, power, and knowing. Anyone can tap into and receive this realm, but it requires surrender to the Divine mystery. You have been building energetic and receptive muscles to sustain an uninterrupted flow of this kind of wisdom for quite a while now.

Didn't you recently write down a goal to feel what it was like to channel?

I did. I wrote that down in my journal as one of my goals about six months ago. I forgot about that.

But I didn't. Now here it is, manifested. Right now, that is what you are doing. Congratulations.

That's it?

> Yes. Nothing more is required. This ability will always be with you because you have mastered a higher level of receptivity. You can ask anything you want. If you become receptive enough, you will hear the answer from the Infinite dimension of You. The Infinite dimension will always offer the perfect solution. It's only a question of whether you are receptive enough.
>
> You can tell it is not the small you are talking to now, right?

Yes, and you are talking way too fast for my small mind to butt in and stop the flow.

> Good thing! We've been communicating for a lot longer than this writing retreat. Your previous book, Divine Breadcrumbs, contains instances where you heard this voice and received insight. That book, in many ways, is the prequel to this book. It reminded you of what it takes to become open to experience enlightenment.

Is it helpful if I ask to channel my spirit guides, or is communicating with the expanded dimension of me enough?

> Notice how your mind always wants more, better, grander.

I see your point. But this is a lot to take in. How are you giving me the exact words to write down?

The English language is a skill in the dimension of the Earth Suit. I'm sending a signal that your mind translates into words. You are transcribing words that are being translated at the same time. It's happening like an orchestra concerto. You and me are connected, perceiving experience from different dimensions. I don't look through a contracted Earth Suit. I see reality differently than you perceive it through your ego-mind's eyes.

Does my voice have a similar sense of humor to yours?

Yes.

It's because you are an energetic extension of me. I'm answering questions that come from your consciousness. You are a practical, funny, and internally focused person, so my voice gives you that kind of information.

I like that I am an energetic extension of you. One of my teachers says, "You are an extension of non-physical Source energy."

That's a great understanding. Imagine looking up at a star in the sky. It looks like a single star. But if you look at it from another angle, it consists of trillions upon trillions of molecules bound together. You could also look at one human body. It is in one form, just one body, but from another perspective, it's made up of trillions of cells.

The fundamental essence of You is not a separate body, separate mind, or separate soul. You are like one massive star made up of trillions of molecules. You are a collection of radiant energies coming into your body to live this life. You are an extension of the brightest energy you can imagine. You are hooked up to the entire grid of the galaxy and beyond. This is where words can never do justice to the immensity of who you are.

That's beautiful, but . . . how can I be sure I'm not making this up?

You're not making this up. Anyone can receive their higher-dimensional self. You can practice this level of receptivity until you sustain a strong connection for extended periods. The longer you abide in this expanded realm, the closer you get to the next gateway of spiritual awakening. Receptivity ushers you through the portal. On the other side is unshakable inner peace because you will know who and what you are and that you can never be harmed. You've been training for this for quite a while. This portal was meant to open for you in Hawaii. Everything in your past has led up to this moment due to your intense focus on your spiritual awakening. This was an inevitable communion.
Other humans shy away from a solid connection with their higher-dimensional selves. They might succeed staying away for a while, but the pull toward receptivity and experiencing higher dimensions of oneself will happen. It's inevitable because the spiritual impulse underlies everything. Even when someone continues to say no to being receptive and instead only relies on their human powers to create their life, they will eventually get in the boat and enjoy the Divine current. It just might

not be this year or this human lifetime.

You, my dear, are in the current. This book appeared, and you received it. But before your ego gives you a pat on the back, you have said no to this flow plenty of times. You said no in small ways to us every few hours of this writing process. You feared the unknown. Your ego got in the way. Stay humble and know beyond any doubt that anyone can do this if they desire.

My favorite experience in writing this book was when you sent the message through every cell of my body that I was not alone, and you would never leave me.

I send messages in all sorts of ways.

I have often heard someone say that your Divine Source will never abandon you. That made sense intellectually, but I didn't feel the truth through my body. Thanks to you, something happened at a cellular level, and I will never forget that my Divine Source is with me always.

Sorry to break it to you, my dear, but you will forget it. You'll have a few more moments of feeling abandoned, but it doesn't matter. You know how to return to the truth. You may sometimes forget who and what you are, but there's no going back. This experience will never be denied. You are forever changed. You are expanding, as you have always been.

Am I supposed to be writing more books with You?

Why would you want to write a book from your small strategic mind again?

Good point.

> This is the first installment in a series of conversations we'll have on spiritual awakening. What you are about to go through will blow your mind, and it will be fun to record our discussion while it happens.
> How do you feel about that?

I'm a little nervous, but more excited than anything. I feel hope and happiness—and much more settled than when I started writing a few days ago.

> This will be a fantastic long-term partnership. Your fear of abandonment can release its pattern now, as you will never abandon yourself. It's impossible.

I can't describe how amazing that feels when you say that.

> You will not only become a brighter star as we continue our journey together, but you will support others to become brighter stars. The world is only getting brighter and more radiant. It is balancing in many ways, and sometimes in the balancing, it feels like it's getting darker, but it's not. It is evolution at play. It's natural for things to regress so they can find the path of expansion that will genuinely be sustainable for everyone and everything. Don't let the regressions or contractions concern you. Everything is expanding. You are growing, and insights are coming to people thick and fast.

I'd love to give you a final way to end this book, but you are so good at writing, so how would you end this writing retreat?

Well, it's been quite a ride. This healing journey has shown me where I am open to receiving and where I still resist. Thank you for being with me and sticking in there when I was afraid. I love the feeling of having your steady companionship on this journey. I am forever grateful.

The feeling is mutual.

Are you sure there is nothing else you want to tell me?

You are an eager student, aren't you?

I guess so.

There is so much more that will come later. I am proud of you because you let me take you somewhere. It was a considerable risk to let go into the unknown. I am proud because, in surrender, you have expanded into the next level of consciousness, which is what you wanted. I am proud of you because you kept up with the process. You owned your projections; you owned your fears. You took time to feel your resistance when it was staring you in the face. You followed my voice and wrote with precision.
Your work is only going to get better from here. The insights you will facilitate for others will be enormous. You have no idea yet.

Keep returning to this mantra: *"I am love, I am joy, I am bliss, I am open, I am receptive, I am now, I need nothing, but I'm ready and available for anything."*
Do you like that mantra?

I do. I am overflowing with love. My heart is bursting. Tears are flowing.

Hawaii is a spiritual activation site for you. You are here on the Islands for another 13 days. Stay open and receive the magic.

I will! We have two days of downtime to relax and swim with the dolphins and turtles. Then, we make our way to the Big Island, my favorite of all the Islands.

The Big Island is younger and more spacious. The volcano is erupting as we speak.

I know. We are flying in as most are evacuating.

That's what the spiritual path is like. You run toward the tiger's mouth while others run away.

The Big Island might be an intense place to be right now.

It will be the perfect place for your awakening.

Contemplative Question:
What does the higher-dimensional You want to share with you?

Access this chapter's guided practice in the *Unshakable Inner Peace* course at: UnshakableSeries.com

THE CONVERSATION CONTINUES

After the writing retreat was over, rest and receptivity were the only things on my to-do list. I walked to a magnificent Banyan tree near where we stayed and basked in its mystery. I had a massage from the guy the ladies in our group called 'God.' Rumor was that his hands could take you to another dimension. He wasn't Datta, but he was close. No need to tell my husband I said that. As the sun descended to Hawaiian music on constant shuffle throughout the resort, I flicked back through some pages of my conversation with The Voice, my higher self.

I was struck by how terrified I was of my readers' judgment, which seems funny now, since we're on this journey together. We are all adventurers of the inner domain, wanting to explore our potential.

Somehow or other, this book found its way into your life. You've read to the last page. We're connected now. That is no accident.

It was no accident the writing retreat was just months after I received my intention for enlightenment. It allowed me to marinate in the juices of such a necessary investigation. It was no accident that Datta challenged me with his skepticism. It invited me to see my closure and fears. It was no accident that I was scheduled to lead retreats on the Big Island directly after writing these pages. It gave me space to stay receptive.

The story doesn't end here. The gifts and shifts from writing this book were like a drop in the ocean compared to what happened after I landed on the Big Island. What unfolded was more than my eruption of terror in front of the beautiful Japanese women who had gathered there and held space for me. I started to have unexplainable visions. I had higher-dimensional experiences while facilitating others. The momentum to higher forms of bliss continued. I felt reborn in some way. It was an awakening of immense proportion.

Unshakable Love, book two in this series, tells what transpired next. Afraid that this ecstatic altered reality would soon fade, I turned to the voice of my higher-dimensional self for advice to try to get this new stage of consciousness to stick. I'd like to say the next phase was all love, light, and giggles, but as you'll discover, there were more fears to excavate and insights to land before another level of awakening could occur.

I've noticed an addiction to the mental realm in spiritual communities. We try to understand things versus experience them. It's why the descent into the body, fears, and feelings are just as important as the ascent into more expanded realms of awareness. People often use spiritual workshops and practices as entertainment. Who can blame us? It's fun to ponder all of this. They can bring us some relief for a while. But everlasting liberation comes after you dare to look at what you don't want to look at. Freedom finds you when you run directly into the tiger's mouth.

Don't be scared. Waiting for you is an extraordinary experience of life on the other side. Your connection to higher-dimensional information and conversations with the Big You lives there.

If you stare into a tiger's mouth, it feels like it's your last moment. But just like death, surrendering your mind to the unknown is not an end. It's a portal to a new beginning. That's what writing this book did for me. Completing this book cleared up my confusion about many spiritual topics and finally pulled me through to a new realm—where I was shocked to discover my identity would soon be torn into pieces.

TO BE CONTINUED . . .

WHO NEEDS TO READ THIS?

Do you know someone who might benefit from reading *Unshakable Inner Peace*? Are you connected to anyone who loves conversations on spirituality, mindfulness, and being a better human?

This book could be a gift for someone who gracefully lives life and is eager for deeper spiritual understanding or for someone who struggles to get off the mental and emotional rollercoaster and needs some extra support. If anyone comes to mind, would you tell them about *Unshakable Inner Peace* or possibly buy them a copy?

Would you also consider writing a review on the platform you purchased this book while it's fresh in your mind? I would be incredibly grateful. Reviews are essential for a small enterprise like ours. Reviews significantly affect how many people see the book on Amazon, Barnes and Noble, or other platforms. If you bought this book directly from me, drop me a line and let me know your experience from reading the book. I'd love to hear from you. My email is: RachaelJayne@TheAwakenedSchool.com.

I'm sure you have many items on your to-do list competing for your attention, and I know it's a huge favor to ask. I would deeply appreciate you sharing and leaving a review.

Much love,
Rachael Jayne

RECOMMENDED RESOURCES

Unshakable Inner Peace: Companion course to this book

Through the experience of writing this book, I realized the profound importance of contemplative questions and embodiment practices. Given that, I created a companion course I'm offering at no cost to you to guide you through an experience of the messages being relayed in each chapter. Join me for spiritual contemplation, meditations, and challenges as you deepen your spiritual awakening experience. UnshakableSeries.com

Retreats with Rachael Jayne

I'm here for support when you want guidance or time to go within. Maybe we'll write together in one of our writing retreats or help build your transformational business at one of The Awakened Business School events. The topics explored in this book are found in my *Unshakable Certainty* and *Open to Receive* retreats.

Join us at Casa Sagrada, our retreat center in Colorado, or through our virtual platform.

Art of Feminine Presence® and *Art of Masculine Presence®* are trainings referred to in this book because they contain potent practices to help sustain the presence necessary for spiritual awakening to accelerate. This work is also about amplifying your magnetic presence so you will be seen and heard the way you want. It's about being unshakable no matter what comes your way.

Check our calendar of events and choose a retreat that calls you: TheAwakenedSchool.com/Calendar.

The Awakened School® has many programs, courses, and live retreats. This is the company that Rachael Jayne and Datta founded in 2009. It hit the Inc. 5000 list in 2019 (America's fastest-growing private companies). All our social media channels are listed there. Become a free member of The Awakened School and participate in our free masterclasses at: TheAwakenedSchool.com

Unshakable Transformation™

If you want to go deep into the three developmental areas covered in Chapter Nineteen that create lasting transformation in your everyday life—Psychology, Somatic Awareness, and Spirituality—you can dive straight into an all-access pass for everything I teach in these realms over 18 months. If you're like me, when I believe something is truly transformative, I want to go all the way as fast as possible. Unshakable Transformation is this opportunity.

Speaking Engagements and Podcast Interviews

I provide keynotes and interactive workshops that range from intimate group settings to packed auditoriums. I work with organizations looking to create a culture where individuals feel seen, heard, and supported. I encourage people to get present, reflect on what's holding them back, and how they can create a life of inner peace and outer purpose. I can speak on the material in this book, or present on my corporate or entrepreneurial conference speaking topics, which are listed at: RachaelJayne.com

ACKNOWLEDGMENTS

The voice of infinite wisdom described in this book appeared during one of our writing retreats at The Awakened School. This particular one was facilitated by our good friend Tom Bird. He led us into the realm of receptivity to our Divine selves and the author within. Thank you, Tom, for challenging me to write from a surrendered place, not a strategic one.

To our team at The Awakened School. Each and every one of you is a class act. Thank you for always going above and beyond for Datta and me and for creating a safe space for our clients to do their inner and outer work. Your laughter and love for each other inspire me to raise the bar as a leader because you all deserve leadership that allows you to excel and enjoy your work.

To all the members of The Awakened School community—whether you've participated in a free masterclass or have been through every program of ours four times—you are more than clients to me. You are my soul family. Thank you for the love you pour on me. An even bigger thanks for showing up for yourself. When we sit together, you show me what awakening really means.

As this book was coming to completion, it was important to have some beta readers. Thank you, Denise Bonanni, Jessica Connor Kennedy, Batoul Hammoud, and Amy Kennedy, for generously giving your time and focus to help ensure this conversation would be clear and benefit others.

I couldn't just have any old editor for a subject matter like this.

I am blessed to be married to a world-class writer and editor who is spiritually grounded and highly intuitive. Datta Groover, you have polished and clarified this conversation without changing the integrity of the message. Your skill and patience have taken my writing to a new realm. Even through our occasionally challenging conversations, you have unconditionally supported me through every single moment since our first kiss. I never imagined I would feel this loved.

Finally, to my unwavering voice that blesses my personal and professional life. Please, keep reminding me of who I really am.

ABOUT THE AUTHOR

Rachael Jayne Groover is the co-founder and CEO of The Awakened School®, which offers transformational experiences for those seeking inner peace and outer purpose. Her work is for those committed to their personal and spiritual awakening, who want to be part of an elevated conversation on human potential and making a positive difference through doing work they love.

She is the creator of retreats such as *Art of Feminine Presence®, Art of Masculine Presence®, Unshakable Certainty,* and *Open to Receive,* which are based on information received in this book.

As a sought-after speaker and trainer on mindfulness, leadership, and conscious entrepreneurship, she also works with business owners and teams who want to create an energy of love, potential, and connection at their events or in their workplace.

Rachael Jayne and Datta's home is in the hills outside Loveland, Colorado. They live with their corgi companion Maya, and Sophie, their faithful rottweiler. Close by is their retreat center, Casa Sagrada.